Sorted!

John McGuire grew up in Sandycove, Co. Dublin, the son of the local headmaster and a medical secretary. He is the second of their five children. His first job was delivering milk after he harassed the milkman into giving him a part-time job. He is now the chairman of four successful companies, which range from hospitality to financial services.

Sorted! is John McGuire's first book. His mother thinks it's deadly. So, who knows, there may be more.

Sorted!

How to Survive and Thrive
When Money is Tight

JOHN MCGUIRE

PENGUIN
IRELAND

PENGUIN IRELAND

Published by the Penguin Group
Penguin Ireland, 25 St Stephen's Green, Dublin 2, Ireland
(a division of Penguin Books Ltd)
Penguin Books Ltd, 80 Strand, London WC2R ORL, England
Penguin Group (USA) Inc., 375 Hudson Street, New York, New York 10014, USA
Penguin Group (Australia), 250 Camberwell Road, Camberwell, Victoria 3124, Australia
(a division of Pearson Australia Group Pty Ltd)
Penguin Group (Canada), 90 Eglinton Avenue East, Suite 700, Toronto, Ontario, Canada M4P 2Y3
(a division of Pearson Penguin Canada Inc.)
Penguin Books India Pvt Ltd, 11 Community Centre, Panchsheel Park, New Delhi – 110 017, India
Penguin Group (NZ), 67 Apollo Drive, Rosedale, Auckland 0632, New Zealand
(a division of Pearson New Zealand Ltd)
Penguin Books (South Africa) (Pty) Ltd, 24 Sturdee Avenue, Rosebank, Johannesburg 2196, South Africa

Penguin Books Ltd, Registered Offices: 80 Strand, London WC2R ORL, England

www.penguin.com

First published 2012
1

Copyright © John McGuire, 2012

The moral right of the author has been asserted

Set in 14/16pt Garamond MT Std
Typeset by Jouve (UK), Milton Keynes
Printed in Great Britain by Clays Ltd, St Ives plc

A CIP catalogue record for this book is available from the British Library

ISBN: 978-1-844-88241-0

www.greenpenguin.co.uk

Penguin Books is committed to a sustainable
future for our business, our readers and our
planet. This book is made from paper certified
by the Forest Stewardship Council.

I'd better dedicate this to Karen,
otherwise she'll kill me.

Contents

	Introduction	ix
1	I'm Drowning in Debt	1
2	I'm Completely Broke	23
3	I've Lost My Job	35
4	My Job is on the Line	51
5	My Business Has Folded	61
6	I Need a New Job	83
7	I Need a New Career	101
8	I Want to be Self-Employed	113
9	I Want to Live to be 100	137
10	I Want to Buy a House	153
11	I Want to Buy Another House	173
12	I Need to Find Low-Risk, High-Yield Investments	191
13	I Need to Protect What I've Got	211
	Good Luck	221
	Acknowledgements	223

Introduction

I used to think I had the mental strength to deal with whatever life could throw at me. I needed less sleep than almost anyone else, I worked harder, I was fitter, I was mentally tougher. I would do things other people were not prepared to do, just to prove a point. At the starting line of the Berlin Marathon, I chain-smoked five cigarettes while rubbing Tiger Balm in my legs. You should have seen the faces on the Germans – me with my Irish flag and a smoke in my mouth.

Earlier that year, me and two friends ran the Rome Marathon. We got there late because we were having our good-luck smoke, and had to run for twenty minutes just to get to the starting line. When we got there, the marathon had already started. So we took off anyway, but found out ages later that we were actually on the Fun Run which was going in the opposite direction. So we ran back and started again. The most depressing sign I ever saw was the '5K' sign after we had been running for about 15K and an hour and a half, but we still managed to finish it. I had raised money for charity and there was no way I was going back to say I had made a mistake. I remember saying to my friend Conor, after we had all stopped blaming each other, 'If we finish this, we will be laughing about it for the rest of our lives.'

Afterwards, we had a quick wash, went for a pizza and proceeded to drink Rome dry for three days. I guess my point is I knew I was mentally tough. I used to joke that only two things would survive a nuclear winter. Cock-roaches and me.

Crash

I set up a mortgage brokerage, First Credit, in 2002, when I was twenty-nine. By 2007, I had acquired numerous prop-erties, and First Credit was organizing over €130 million in mortgages a year and was making a gross profit of over €1.4 million a year. I had just invested in two new com-panies, I had a net worth north of €10 million and I was making a decent year's salary every month.

Then came the crash. Boom. The pendulum swung. By 2010 I was worth minus €4 million and was losing €10,000 to €15,000 every month for nearly two years. I had seen a 95 per cent collapse in my main company and therefore my main income. I had become a millionaire early on, then a multi-millionaire in my mid-thirties. I know what it's like to make a million euros in a day, I know what it's like to lose ten times that almost overnight. I know what it's like to stare at the ceiling every night for months and months on end, unable to sleep because you can't balance the books.

When the offer came through to write this book, I was having the crap beaten out of me by the recession. Every week I was on the ropes fighting for my business life. I felt like a boxer who had taken on too many fights. When you're in uncharted territory and the owner of a business that has suffered spectacular declines, you have to wonder if writing a book is a good idea. What if I fail halfway through writing it? Or worse, just after it comes out? I've seen other businessmen of my age get involved in projects like this, only to find their businesses in receivership a few weeks later. I remember thinking, 'How can I get involved in a project like this when my business is still in such grave danger?'

Taking Responsibility

But I decided I would do whatever I had to to survive. I refused to go into arrears and become part of the problem. I took it head-on and continued to invest in new companies. No one forced me to make these decisions. I've taken big gambles that have worked spectacularly well for me. So what happens when the tide turns? Do I just go, 'Hey, it's not my fault. There is nothing I can do. It's the recession'?

For me and people like me, we are either part of the solution or part of the problem. If I can't make my loan repayments then I'm part of the problem and half the reason our country is in the mess it's in. I don't think it's right to take on the responsibility of an employer and a major borrower and accept the riches from the good times, but not be prepared to do everything an average person would not do to keep things afloat. An average person did not make millions in assets and earn a decent year's salary in a month.

My focus through 2009 and 2010 was survival, plain and simple. Try to get back to profitability and replace my businesses that were decimated with new ones that would survive and thrive in this new Ireland we're now living in.

So I took it on, I fought it. I invested and I survived, I hope, but for two years I just worked. I didn't read a book or pick up the guitar or do anything that was good for the soul. For most of 2009 I was able to keep positive and keep fighting, but then at some stage the realization came that this was the new normal. Since then and up until recently, I've done very little of note on a personal level, unless you can count annoying your girlfriend (which is quite good fun).

I've achieved nothing sport-wise and have spent almost no time with my friends. I didn't do as much living as I'd usually fit into two years. I made the decision to keep investing in new ventures and servicing my debt when I could not afford to do either. The really hard bit is investing and spending money when you're losing money. You question your decisions every single day.

The smart thing would have been to take my spare cash and move to my mortgage-free place in Dubai with its sea view and private beach. The smart thing would have been to shrug my shoulders and say there was nothing I could do. But for me to do that, I would have become a huge part of the problem and chances are I would have felt miserable. Rich, but miserable.

Taking on the Recession

I put my plan together. It involved gambling everything I had on three new companies and two sites that I knew would eventually be profitable. If it didn't work out, it would be game over. You lost. I sold everything that was not nailed down, then reviewed my positions. My monthly income was still at least €10,000 less than I was spending.

I had loads of vacant offices with no takers and I was living in a house that could command between €2,000 and €2,500 per month. The commercial market got hit so hard that that was more than I could get for the top two floors of my Dublin 2 offices. With half my properties vacant or not paying me anything, my mind would not leave me alone.

'Pride comes before a fall,' I kept thinking . . . So I advertised my home for €2,300 and decided if anyone paid me €2,000, I'd take it. I'd accept that it was the right thing to do and I'd move out. But if I was offered less than €2,000, the universe was telling me to stay put. Two weeks later I got an offer of €1,950. No deal. I wouldn't budge on the price. Three weeks later, someone else offered me €2,000. I don't think I have ever been so dejected to get an offer on a property. But I had made a deal with fate. So I rented out my house, moved into one of my vacant offices and worked on rebuilding what had fallen. I spent the guts of 2010 living in a 200-odd-square-foot room with no kitchen, that I basically converted into a bedsit. I guess I made it cosy enough. I moved out the office furniture and replaced it with a TV, couches and a mattress. Could have been worse; at least it wasn't a Holiday Inn.

Stress

I spent 2009 staring at the ceiling, trying to work out what to do. Whether to liquidate First Credit or to keep it going. I still had very loyal staff but the income of the company was always less than the outgoings, and when it came to the end of the month I would have to withdraw savings to pay the shortfall in my mortgages, loans and business expenses. The stress started to really take its toll towards the end of the year. By Friday evening I would need four or five drinks before I could relax enough to talk. The only people I really wanted to meet were my brother Mike or Karen, my girlfriend. They were the only ones who'd let me say nothing until I could relax enough to talk. It felt like having a clamp around my brain that I could not release.

I stopped caring about my appearance. I stopped keeping in touch with friends. My brain was skipping around so much, I wasn't able to relax long enough to read a book or watch a movie. A lot of business and property people committed suicide at this time. I can understand the dark places your mind can get to when this unrelenting pressure is there and you can't see a way out. Add to the mix a €10-million insurance policy sitting in the bank, six months or a year without a proper night's sleep, a few children, school fees coming in, and the mind can start to see things in grey that are actually black and white. I'm not saying I was considering it, but I understand it and how it could look like an option at your darkest hour, especially if you are the patriarch of a family.

Tougher than Everyone?

I thought I was tougher than everyone, but when you take away a man's income, his car and his home, it can chip away at your confidence. And it started to wear me down. I started calling the office I'd moved into 'the cell'.

'I'm going back to solitary,' I used to joke. Most of the time I was confident about what I was doing, but sometimes my head would get the better of me. 'Well fucking done, you champion. How the fuck did you manage to piss away €15 million? Well done! Thirty-seven years of age, insolvent and living in a fucking office.'

All I did was work and sleep. My office was next door so I would 'come home', sit down, then think of something and go back to my desk. My head never really got a break, and all the time I was losing around €15,000 per month. Looking back now, the hardest part of it was not getting any sort of a break. As the office and home were essentially the same thing, I never got away from it.

The Corner Turned

I can say now with some degree of certainty that for the moment anyway, I have survived the recession. It took a severe toll on me. It has taken two years that I will never get back. They aren't wasted because I've survived, but I don't feel I have lived them. I survived them. They were two years of the most awful stress; stress I could not even imagine and never thought for one minute might apply to me. One thing they did give me is the credibility to give advice on things I wish I'd known more about when the crash happened. It's true what they say. You do learn more from your mistakes than from the things you get right.

I now have a thriving commercial insurance brokerage called Pembroke Insurances. First Credit no longer specializes in mortgages. It's now First Credit Insurance. Quotedevil. ie is my online low-cost car, home, van and health insurance provider. This company, I believe, will be my biggest ever. It already has 10,000 customers after a year and a half of trading. I've opened the nicest bar in Dublin: Dax Café Bar, which is First Credit's old boardroom. So I am back to doing what I do best.

The day we opened the bar we had fifteen customers. The next day I walked in and could not get a seat. All my plans started falling into place within weeks of each other. My sites were finished, I rented everything, and all of the companies started taking off at the same time. I went from losing money and having one part-time employee to creating over twenty-five new jobs in a couple of months. I have forty staff now, and expect to create at least another twenty jobs over the next six to nine months. Hopefully, I'll get back to paying myself a decent salary, too! These are the reasons I decided to accept the offer to write this book.

I have seen the good, the bad and the damned ugly and lived to tell the tale. I hope to be able to impart some of the lessons I have learned to you. And let me say this. I firmly believe that we are now being presented with the greatest opportunity of our lifetime, if we only have the balls to take it.

1

I'm Drowning in Debt

Here's the first and most important thing to say: there is a way out of this. You are not the first person to have found yourself drowning in debt and you won't be the last. It is possible to stop the letters and the phone calls and deal with things in a way that's fair to both you and your creditors. There is a definite, structured way of dealing with the fact that you can no longer afford your commitments. The steps I'll go through here have been taken by millions of people before you.

I've been that person. I was stuck on fixed rates of over 5 per cent when the crash happened, then I got moved onto even higher repayments when I could not afford it. When my mortgage business collapsed, my company went from being a relatively large enterprise to one that wasn't even able to pay me. Also, because my main investments were property, my net worth dropped by around €15 million, so I was worth minus millions. Like so many other people, I was in negative equity, only on a bigger scale.

This is going to sound strange, but I was okay with the fact that I was not worth millions any more. Don't get me wrong, it wasn't great, but if you're an investor or businessman, that's all part of the game. You can't win them all. Man up and move on. The really hard part was that I was losing €10,000 to €15,000 per month, every month. And if you can't service your debt and your debts are called in, you lose your properties. Then it's game over. You will never have the chance to see if they come back, and the deposits, stamp duty and gains you made are wiped out. So it may look worse in print having a big change in your net worth, but it's in the minor league compared to being insolvent; when your income is less than your outgoings. Maybe the stress is greater when the money gets higher but I don't believe that. The only difference is the position of the decimal point.

The reality is that most of us here in Ireland have not been in this situation before. We don't have a history of dealing with personal or business debt, and so we're just not set up for it. In America, bankruptcy is a badge of honour for entrepreneurs. If you're a businessman in America and haven't been bankrupt, what do you know? In Ireland, under current legislation, if you're bankrupt it lasts for twelve years. Twelve years! This is ridiculous. There is, however, light at the end of the tunnel. Legislation due in 2012 will change that, but more about that later.

A Plan

If you've lost your job, if you've had a salary reduction or your partner has lost their job, if you're overextended and you are now unable to meet your commitments, the first thing you need is a plan.

You also need to talk about it. This may sound ridiculous, but it's not. I remember one of the first times I talked about what I had been through. I was completely taken aback by the emotion that came out. I was left asking myself, who is this man? I don't show emotion! That's not me! At the time, I had just come through the toughest part of it and was finally admitting it in a conversation with my girlfriend, Karen. I could feel the tide of emotion coming. It wasn't the major loss in assets. I'd been having a good old laugh at my own expense about that for ages. It was the stress over not making enough to pay my debt and the ever-diminishing cash reserves. The constant fear that I'd end up as one more businessman who ran out of funds.

But once I spoke about it and it was out there, I felt sudden relief. I didn't want to discuss it up until then because I felt I would be worrying people around me. That was stupid, because they were already worrying.

If you are hiding financial problems from your partner, you need to sit them down, maybe have a glass of wine and go through everything with them. It's so important to talk about it and get it out in the open. If you don't, the pressure keeps on building and building. You need to release it.

The process of dealing with not being able to afford your outgoings is simple maths. You just work out what you need to live and pay your mortgage, then divide what is left among your creditors. You've also got to work out which is the most important debt. This gets priority. The mistake so many people make is paying the loans that are not as important. Often, the lender that rings the most gets paid off first, when it's the roof over your head that's the most important thing.

It is simple maths, but the process takes time and commitment and you may not initially get positive responses from some or all of your creditors. You need to allocate enough time to deal with it every month and stick exactly to your word.

MABS

MABS is the state-run Money Advice and Budgeting Service. It's there to help people who are struggling with debt. MABS is the first place to go if you are running into difficulty, though there is a waiting list. Make an appointment, and they will show you how to go about doing everything I'll go through in this chapter. They'll advise you on all areas of dealing with debt, especially dealing with creditors, and won't charge you anything.

Debt Management Companies

Debt management companies are privately owned companies who specialize in this area of business. If you are going to use one of these, you have to be VERY, VERY careful and do a lot of research first. It's an unregulated area; you don't need any experience to set up a debt management company. This does not mean that they are all bad, but it's very important to find out about their fees and experience before instructing them. You'll hear enough phone calls to radio shows complaining about these guys to know that there are bad eggs among them.

There is a body called the Debt Management Association of Ireland (*www.dmai.ie*). They have a code of conduct for their members, so this is a good place to start. The standard fee will range between €400 and €800, plus there's always a small monthly retainer. The downside of dealing with a debt management company is, of course, the fee, and the fact that they are unregulated. This means you have no one to complain to, and there's no one who can force binding decisions on them. So proceed with caution.

The upside is that you have someone dealing with all of your creditors, so you pay one monthly fee rather than sending out a number of cheques each month.

Here's the other consideration. By the time it gets to this stage, the stress can have taken its toll and the idea of someone else taking responsibility for everything can be extremely attractive. I'm personally doing this for a friend at the moment, simply because they just do not have the energy to learn how it all works. In my mind, a brother or sister, a friend or partner who is good at this type of thing, in consultation with MABS and the strategy I've written about here, is a better option than a debt management company if at all possible.

Three Steps

There are three steps to getting yourself out of debt:

1) Prepare your household budget, including your mortgage or rent
2) Prioritize your debts
3) Negotiate with creditors.

Prepare Your Household Budget

First, you need to work out your exact income. The best way of doing this is with an Excel spreadsheet. I have shown on pages 11–13 what a typical financial statement should look like. You can also get a copy from my website *www.johnmcguire.ie.*

When you're working out your income, you need to include everything, including child benefit and any income from, say, room rental. Also, make sure you are in receipt of all of your entitlements from welfare, such as mortgage interest supplement, voluntary contributions or any additional payments from social welfare, as well as tax refunds such as mortgage interest relief, relief on service charges and medical tax relief.

Once you have worked out your exact income, the next step is working out your exact budget. It takes a little time, but you need to use the same spreadsheet and include everything you spend, from daily expenses such as lunch, to annual expenses such as motor tax and TV licence. And absolutely everything in between. Your partner needs to do the same. The first expenditure to start with is your mortgage or rent payment, as this secures the roof over your head.

You need to be very honest. Include everything, and while you're at it, thoroughly assess your spending. If there's money going on nights out, but you still expect your creditors to accept lower payments, you really need to cop on. Your creditors will not accept this and you will have no credibility negotiating reduced payments if parts of your spending are found to be exaggerated.

When the time comes, the more honesty you approach your lenders with, the greater the likelihood they will accept your proposals. Pick a day once a month to review your income and expenditure. If anything comes up that night, you are not available! Use this exercise to fully control your finances and to revise your income and expenditure to see if you need to amend it. Once you have this finished, you have a full assessment of exactly what it costs you to live each month. If the money left over is substantially less than your monthly loan repayments, you need to negotiate with your lenders for reduced payments. Before you get to that stage, however, you're going to need to prioritize your debts.

Prioritize Your Debts

This very simply means working out which debts are the most important. The reason for this is that any action taken against you varies, depending on whether the loan you've taken out is secured or unsecured. An example of a secured debt is a mortgage or car finance. Unsecured is a credit card or store card. Secured finance means that the loan is secured against an item that can be repossessed, whereas with unsecured credit, it cannot.

Your repayment mortgage or rent is your number one priority. The next thing you need to do is to prioritize the remaining debt. This could include arrears on mortgage or rent, hire-purchase car finance and secured home-improvement loans. These get priority over the remaining loans you have as the lender can enforce repossession or eviction if the repayments are not maintained.

9

Utility arrears (electricity, gas, etc.) should be included as priority debts, as non-payment can result in your service being disconnected. Negotiate with all of these creditors first. Offer repayments that are reasonable but will allow you to maintain your household expenditure. If at all possible, maintain the correct repayment on all secured finance.

Most importantly, don't put your head in the sand. You will be amazed by how much better you will feel by tackling all of this head on. Never ignore the letters or phone calls. Deal with them promptly and if you make an arrangement, stick to it at all costs. Never make promises you won't be able to keep.

I know one woman who didn't open her post for a year because every time she did, it was another demand for repayment. She found it almost impossible to deal with the strain. She used to confide in her next-door neighbour, who was in a similar position. They'd have trouble holding back the tears when discussing their finances. Then one of them got herself together and found an agent to represent her. She put in place a plan like the one I've been describing, and soon afterwards her neighbour did the same. A few weeks later, when everything was bedded down, they got a couple of bottles of wine, collected a year's worth of unopened post and put it all in a heap in the back garden. They sat down, opened up the wine, got more than a little tipsy and burnt the lot. They've opened every letter ever since.

Remaining Debt

Once you have these priority debts dealt with, you can deal with the remaining debt (credit cards, store cards, personal loans, etc.). Simply divide equally between your remaining creditors whatever is left after you've looked after your living expenses and priority debts.

Here's an example. Suppose you have €400 left after your household expenditure and your priority debts, but you owe a further €100,000 in outstanding loans. Regardless of what the scheduled repayments are, you only have €400 to spend. So it needs to be split equally, depending on the amount you owe. So if you owe one lender €10,000 and the other €90,000, you offer the first one €40 and the other lender €360. That is all you can afford. Basically, if you owe one bank half of your remaining debt, you pay them half of what's left. If you owe another one a quarter of your remaining debt, you offer them a quarter of what's left, and so on.

SAMPLE FINANCIAL STATEMENT

CURRENT INCOME SUMMARY

Income Statement Details	Monthly Amount (€)	Notes
Net Take Home Salary	€2,350.00	
Net Take Home Salary (Spouse)	€1,100.00	
Child Benefit	€300.00	2 children
Jobseeker's Benefit		
Pension Income		
Rental Income		
Total Income	€3,750.00	

EXPENDITURE/HOUSEHOLD BUDGET

Expenditure Statement Details	Monthly Amount (€)	Notes
Mortgage or Rent Repayment	€1,050.00	
Food and Housekeeping	€635.00	
Electricity	€60.00	
Gas/Oil	€75.00	
Mobile Phone	€60.00	
Telephone	€50.00	
Car Petrol	€180.00	2 cars
Car Service	€45.00	
Car Insurance	€60.00	
Car Tax	€70.00	
Childcare	€200.00	Montessori
Medical/Dental	€40.00	
Clothing/Laundry	€80.00	
Pets	€25.00	1 dog, 1 cat
TV Licence	€15.00	
School Meals/Meals at Work	€90.00	
Sports, Hobbies and Entertainment	€50.00	Gym membership as advised by doctor
Broadband/Internet	€30.00	
Sky/Cable	€35.00	
Refuse Collection	€26.00	

Expenditure Statement Details	Monthly Amount (€)	Notes
Total Expenditure	€2,876.00	
Disposable Income (what is left)	€874.00	

Disposable Income: Total Income (€3,750) minus Total Expenditure (€2,876) = €874
Note: When working out the monthly equivalent of a weekly expense, multiply the figure by 52 (weeks) and divide by 12 (months). For example, Weekly Food €135 (€135 multiply by 52 divide by 12 = €585 per month). Multiplying by four does not work as there are thirteen four-weekly periods in a year.

Now, here are the priority debts to be resolved out of the €874 left after the mortgage and housekeeping:

PRIORITY DEBT

Priority Debt	Monthly Amount (€)	Notes
3 Months' Mortgage Arrears (€4,400.00)	€200.00	Agreement to clear arrears over 22 months
Hire Purchase on Car (Arrears €600.00)	€250.00	Repayment plus €50.00 to clear arrears
Total Priority Debt Repayment	€450.00	

After the household budget is paid and the priority debt is taken care of, there is €424 left (that's disposable income of €874 less €450 for priority debt detailed above). You now have to negotiate with the unsecured creditors to work out a way of fairly distributing this leftover sum between them. The first rule is to be fair to all your creditors, otherwise any negotiation is bound to fail. Secondly, the proposed repayment should reflect the balance owing on the debt, not the contractual repayment.

Here is how our example looks, taking all non-priority creditors into consideration (remember our remaining disposable income of €424 per month):

NON-PRIORITY DEBT

Creditor Name	Balance (€)	Contracted Repayment (€)	Proposed Repayment (€)
Bank Loan	€11,000.00	€279.50	€204.56
Credit Card Co.	€2,500.00	€120.00	€46.50
Credit Union	€6,000.00	€177.00	€111.57
Bank Credit Card	€3,300.00	€155.00	€61.37
Totals	€22,800.00	€731.50	€424.00

The proposed repayments that you now offer your unsecured creditors are calculated as a percentage of the disposable income you now have. To work out the percentages, take the amount owed, divide by the total debt and multiply by 100.

So, in the case of the credit card debt, that's €2,500.00 divided by €22,800 and multiplied by 100, which gives 10.96%. You are now going to offer this lender 10.96% of the amount you have available to pay. That's €424.00 × 10.96% = €46.50.

Negotiate with Creditors

Now that you have formulated your plan, it's time to negotiate. Send each creditor your detailed household budget, together with details of your proposed payment plan. Remember, in all your dealings with creditors, be sure to keep detailed records of your correspondence and telephone conversations. That way, if they decline your proposals and issue proceedings for judgement, you will have a detailed file with which to defend the action. In your letter, ask for interest and penalty charges to be frozen or reduced, even temporarily. You may not be successful with all your creditors but one of the most important pieces of advice I can give you is to make a payment to them even if they do not agree on your plan. In addition, enclose a letter explaining that you simply cannot afford the original repayment as per the plan dated, e.g. 01/01/2011, and could they please reduce the repayment to what you can afford, as per the new plan. It is vital that you are seen as someone who is trying to pay as opposed to someone who is not willing to pay. After three or six months you will find most if not all creditors will agree to the revised/affordable repayment. This does work, but I have to admit I was still worried about the banks not accepting the spreadsheet and proposed repayments I worked out for the friend I am negotiating for. However, one week later, I got letters back accepting the proposal as it was obvious there was no more money to pay once the expenditure sheet came in. Strangely enough, debt collection agencies can be easier to deal with than the banks themselves, as they have more experience in dealing with people in these circumstances.

Sample Letters

Here's a sample letter offering reduced repayment on a stressed debt.

XXX Bank Ltd
1 Main Street
Dublin 2

1st January 2011
Account Number: 12345

Dear Sirs,

I am writing to advise you that since making the above agreement with you, my financial circumstances have changed. My income has fallen dramatically due to cutbacks within the organization where I work, and reductions to the child benefit which my family receives.

I have enclosed a detailed income and expenditure sheet which shows the impact on my disposable income of these reductions. As a consequence, I must ask you to accept a reduced payment of €105.56 per month until such time as I can increase this amount. Please note that I have requested all my creditors to accept similar reductions and have enclosed details of all of my debts and proposed payments.

I would also request that you refrain from adding further interest or penalties to my account in order to allow my repayments to reduce the outstanding debt as quickly as possible. To facilitate this new arrangement, please send me a revised standing order mandate.

I intend to review all my household expenses in the hope of freeing up additional disposable income to repay my debt.

I look forward to hearing from you.

Yours faithfully,
Joe Murphy
1 Main Street

Here's an example of a letter you could send if you have no additional disposable income after priority expenditure and priority debt.

ABC Bank Ltd
1 Main Street
Dublin 2

1st January 2011
Account Number: 12345678

Dear Sirs,

I am writing to advise you that since making the above agreement with you, my financial circumstances have changed. My income has been dramatically reduced due to cutbacks within the organization where I work and reductions to the child benefit which we receive. In addition, my wife has lost her job and is not entitled to any redundancy payment.

I have enclosed a detailed income and expenditure sheet which shows the impact of these events on my disposable income. As you can see, I have no money left to pay my creditors. As a consequence, I must ask you to accept a token payment of €10.00 per month until such time as I can increase this amount.

Please note that I have asked all my creditors to accept similar reductions and have enclosed details of all of my debts and token payments to all of my creditors. I understand that this amount is very low but it is as much as I can afford at present. I would also request that you refrain from adding further interest or penalties to my account to allow my repayments to reduce the outstanding debt as quickly as possible.

I will contact you as soon as my circumstances change.
I look forward to hearing from you.

Yours faithfully,
Joe Murphy
1 Main Street

Dealing with Bullies

You may not get positive responses from some or all of your creditors initially, but it's still important to make a payment to them, because it shows that you are making every reasonable effort to deal with your obligations. But because there's no legislation in this area, lenders do have to agree to your proposals. They can and do play hardball, sending back the cheques and looking for full payment. Just one bank writing back and not agreeing to your plan can knock the confidence out of you. The legislation to deal with all of this, though on its way, is long overdue.

Keep trying to get them to accept a payment, even when it seems there is little point. There will always be companies and lenders out there who will refuse, but keep posting them the cheque each month. These companies prefer the bullying option of ignoring your request and looking for a full payment. The premise they're working off is that they want to get more out of you than your other creditors. This is why, when you are in arrears, some may ring four or five times a day.

One of the big worries people have is that you can end up in jail for non-payment of a debt. If one of your creditors does not agree to your plan they may pursue you, so you need to show that you are paying what you can out of what you have got. That way, if you do end up in court, you can show you have written to them detailing what you earn, what you need to live on, and that you are distributing what you have left proportionally. If you can show the judge that you made every effort to repay your debt out of what you have, you are in a strong position because you are demonstrating that you have not shown 'wilful neglect'. You would have to hope that the judge would see it in the same way any reasonable person would, and that if you are paying everything you have after food and your mortgage, they will not come down on you.

The good news is that, as part of our deal with the IMF, new bankruptcy legislation has to be brought in by the first quarter of 2012. This will give us definitive rules and legislation. The Law Reform Commission produced a report that made extensive recommendations on the whole area of debt and the law. One of the main recommendations is the abolition of imprisonment for debt, regulation for debt collection and holistic debt settlement. It covers most of the areas we have just gone through in this chapter. It is long overdue, but we have to hope that most, if not all, of the recommendations will become law.

Judgements

If your creditors do not agree to your proposals and, especially, if you cannot afford to pay them anything, it's likely they will go to court for a judgement. In my best layman's terms, a judgement is really legal recognition that you owe a person or company money. There are other types of judgement. A judgement mortgage is where the court recognizes the amount you owe, and this is put as a second charge on your property after your mortgage. So, once the property is sold (whenever that may be) and your mortgage is cleared, any remaining proceeds then repay your debt. There are also judgements against your income, where you will be required to pay an amount out of your income to repay your debt.

If you arrive at this situation, you need to prove, using the expenditure sheets, that you have no disposable income to discharge your debt. If you can't afford to pay before you go to court, you can't afford to pay after you go to court. If, however, you have the disposable income but are not paying, that's a different story entirely. As soon as the law gets involved, you really need to talk to the free legal aid people: *www.flac.ie* will help you through this.

Situations like these have happened before and will happen again. In a few years' time, when things are better, you may be able to negotiate a lower settlement than the judgement that was secured against you.

Credit Rating

Another major concern can be your credit rating. Forget your credit rating. It should be the least of your worries. If you are coming to terms with being broke and not able to afford your outgoings, your credit rating is gone, so forget about it. You are not going to be borrowing money over the next few years, anyway. The very last thing you should be worrying about is what the corporations that caused half our problems think of your credit rating, and they are the only ones who check it. You need to realize for the short to medium term that your credit rating is effectively gone.

The banks have no money to lend anyway, and even if they did, the last thing you need is another loan. Securing your home, making sure you've enough to live on and then being fair to your creditors are your priorities now. You can have that fight in a few years' time, but right now, forget about it. When the time comes to borrow again there will be exceptions made for this period in our lives. Right now, it's about being able to wake up without that constant anxiety in your stomach. And if you follow these steps you can get to that point.

2

I'm Completely Broke

There are some people for whom managing money comes really easy. Then there are the rest of us. I'm a spender, not a saver. When I was growing up, we used to get our pocket money on Saturday mornings. There were five of us kids. Me and my younger sister, who was closest to me in age, used to head off down to Robinson's Newsagents in Glenageary to spend our thirty or forty pence, or whatever it was at the time. Caitriona was great with her money even then, and would get enough sweets to last the week. Her trick was to pick particular types of sweets, like chewing gum, or Blackjacks, that would last for ages. That way, she could have some all day Saturday but also give herself little rewards through the week. I thought this was a great idea. There was only one problem. White chocolate mice. I loved white chocolate mice. They cost the same as a Blackjack, they tasted infinitely better, but lasted only a fraction of the time. The most you could get out of a bag of white chocolate mice with my personality type was about four minutes, whereas a bag of Blackjacks could last for hours.

By half-ten on a Saturday morning, I would have an empty plastic bag thoroughly licked clean of any and all white chocolate dust. My little sister, by contrast, would have eaten one piece of chewing gum or one Blackjack and would still be savouring it. I would spend the day ruing my decision to go for the chocolate mice, promising myself that I would not make the same mistake next week and, if truth be known, trying to convince my little sister that it would be a good idea to share. All week, I would promise myself that I would do as she did next time.

When the next Saturday eventually came, after what seemed like a month, we would head down to Robinson's again. All the way down, I would definitely be getting Blackjacks. Caitriona would even be prepping me so I would not be as foolhardy as last week. Open the door . . . up to the counter . . . there they are, a big plastic box of chocolate mice waiting to be eaten. There are the Blackjacks, but you don't love Blackjacks! They're great when you don't have anything else, but . . . 'Can I have . . . agghh . . . thirty chocolate mice, please?'

The allure of those mice was just too strong and I was too weak. I guess I did have four or five minutes of unadulterated pleasure, enjoying the best sweet in the world, but then I'd have a week to think about my decision.

You Are the Problem

Certain people are born with the ability to manage money. They enjoy planning and don't feel happy unless they have the entire month worked out. The rest of us have to learn it. And it is something you have to learn. Earning more money does not sort out the problem. If you are a person who lives outside your means when you are on €20,000, you will be a person who lives outside your means if you are on €200,000. It's just the credit card limit will be higher, the overdraft bill will be higher, and so on. Michael Jackson was earning a couple of million a week and still could not live within his means.

It's easy to blame it on not earning enough, but that is not the problem. You are the problem! Have you ever got a raise and thought, things will be different now that I have a bit more money? The reality is that things usually remain more or less the same. Your spending simply adjusts to your budget so at the end of the month, you're still out of cash as per normal.

When everything started falling down around me in 2009, the thing that was hardest to address was the spending. I don't mean luxury items like holidays or cars, just the day-to-day spending. Food and wine, and so on. You already know you can't blow a couple of grand on something, but the day-to-day money just flies out of your pocket so that you can't work out where it's gone. I found that almost impossible to sort out. So I know how difficult it is. But if you don't sort it out yourself, you are going to lead a life of constant worry.

You have to work out your weekly budget of essentials, from groceries to electricity and everything in between. You are allowed to have a treat each week out of the leftovers, and as hard as it is, you have to stick to that spending habit week in week out. Believe it or not, you can get satisfaction out of controlling your desire to spend. It took me years to realize you can get more enjoyment from the occasional treat than indulging whenever you want. It's almost as satisfying as getting off a Ryanair flight not having bought any of their overpriced crap. When you're sitting on those cramped little seats that don't move, surrounded by garish yellow, a cup of tea or a glass of wine really does help, but I just can't stand the feeling of being ripped off. Three missed flights in one weekend at full price will bring that hatred out in you. Getting to the desk in the airport after missing a Ryanair flight is one horrible feeling.

'Excuse me, Miss, I missed my flight.'

'Okay, Mr McGuire, bend over this table for a moment, we will make this as painful as possible.'

So when I do fly with them I try and spend as little as possible. When I get off the flight having not spent, it's a little moral victory.

Sometimes, even when you've reeled in your spending, the urge to spend breaks out before you can stop yourself, especially if you are someone like me that acts on impulse. As part of my drive to be frugal, I went to Lidl last year. What a great place for a bargain! I can't remember what I went in for but I left twenty minutes later with two guitars, a wrench set, a power tool and a tray full of drinkable yoghurt (don't go for the drinkable yoghurts, they're full of sugar). I left without what I went in for but I still got change from €200.

So, even when you're trying to be good, that urge to spend is always there. These days, one of my guilty pleasures is the Lidl magazine that comes with the Sunday papers. The bargains are so random, from a wetsuit to a lawnmower. You never know what's going to be in it and it's all for half of nothing. I saw an electric drum kit for €139 last week. How can they make it all so cheap?

The Budget

There are two things that need to be addressed if you are broke. Your spending is the first and most difficult thing. The second is your income. As in Chapter One, you need a spreadsheet which fully details your spending. One of the things you'll hear most in relation to budgeting is that people just don't know where their money is going or why they are always broke at the end of each month. So here's how you find out.

There is nothing as boring or as informative as a household budget spreadsheet. You need to use it to record everything you spend, because if you can see where you're spending money, you'll be able to address it. Look in detail at everything the money goes on, from electricity to phone and broadband, entertainment, groceries and schoolbooks.

Shop around. See whether you can go cheaper on absolutely everything. Is there cheaper refuse collection? Can you get cheaper gas and electricity? Broadband? Is public transport a cheaper option? Once you have your budget, you need to stick to it religiously. If your budget for food is €100 a week, don't spend a penny more. If the shopping takes a lot more time because you're checking out the prices on everything, so be it. Far better to spend time on shopping around than on worrying at the end of the week because you didn't. There are different deals going on in supermarkets all the time. Find out what and where they are. Use discount cards in the supermarkets and the two-for-one options whenever they come up. You need to be on the lookout for deals constantly.

And when you have got through the week within your budget, reward yourself with something you like. Pizza and a film for the family, the cinema, a takeaway or a bottle of wine; whatever it is that you can look forward to each week when you are making this extra effort to stay within budget. These treats are important. You can't expect yourself to stay frugal all the time. Drive yourself too hard and your will won't stay the course. You'll end up falling back into old habits. When the reward comes, savour it. And use deal vouchers to get your weekly treat, too. The online deal companies like *www.boards.ie*, *www.livingsocial.com* and *www.groupon.ie* have daily deals offering 60 to 70 per cent off restaurants and everything else you can think of. Offers like these have just exploded in the past two years. There seems to be a new company launching every week. But don't make the mistake a lot of people make: they buy on impulse, then never use the voucher. As a businessman I've used them loads of times to sell things. They're great for a sudden inflow of cash, but a quarter of people buy and never use.

It's Up to You

The harsh reality of all of this is that it's up to you. It all boils down to something I heard years ago: 'If it's going to be, it's up to me.' This did not make much of an impact on me at the time, but twenty years later, looking back, it's clear that whenever there was a seismic change in my luck or my circumstances, it's because *I* made a seismic change. I did not want to work in the kitchen of a restaurant on a

Friday night when I was twenty-one, I did not want to sell my convertible car when I was twenty-three, or rent out all of the rooms in my house when I was twenty-five, and I sure as hell did not want to move into the office at thirty-five years of age.

Each time, I was in a situation where I had to either get into something or get out of something. I knew there was a sacrifice to be made and I decided to endure some short-term pain for a long-term gain. The only person who can make these changes is you.

Material stuff is secondary. What kind of car you drive is secondary. I have no interest in driving a flashy car and being six months down on my payments. Give me the crap car and being up to date any day. Otherwise, you're all fur coat and no knickers. (Though, to be honest, I don't know why this phrase is supposed to suggest something undesirable. I always thought that sounded kinda all right . . .)

Anyway, you can get a nice car when the good times come around again, and they will come around again.

Boosting Income

There is no hard and fast rule for how to start earning more. For me, it was gambling on business success and property. For others, it might be night-time education or promotion, but you need to look at your circumstances and work out what it is that you need to do. Are there short-term solutions? Can you rent out a room? Can you get overtime? Can you get a part-time job?

It may also be worth checking out your entitlements. The best place to check these is on *www.citizensinformation.ie*. There is a range of social welfare payments you may be entitled to, depending on your circumstances, from fuel allowance to back-to-work allowances. Certainly, if you have had a major wage reduction or are self-employed and have had your income seriously compromised, it's going to be very difficult to make ends meet.

Thinking long term, will furthering your education improve your earnings? If not, would furthering your education in a different direction be a wiser option? Is there a more lucrative area of business, a profession or a trade that you can move into? Get onto recruitment company websites and speak to as many people as possible about growth areas. I do my best business when I'm just meeting people. That's when ideas and business pop up. After I converted my boardroom into a bar, more business was done in that exact same room in a few months than in the previous six years. I'm not really doing my job when I'm at my PC. I'm doing my job when I am in meetings and out and about seeing people.

What else can you do? How about simply working harder in your current position in order to get a promotion? Every boss knows who is out the door at a minute past close every day; every boss knows who is prepared to work to get what is needed to be done and who is just looking to do the bare minimum. If you work averagely, expect average results and performance. If you want above-average results, you have to put in above-average effort. The harder you work, the luckier you become.

If you are working extra hard or if your figures are higher

than everyone else's, make sure your boss knows what you are doing and where you want to go. Make sure you PR yourself correctly. There is no point in working extra hard if nobody will ever know. If you work til 8.30 in the evening, send an email just before you go home. If you're in at 7.30 in the morning, send an email the second you arrive. Tell your boss where you want to go in the organization, don't wait for him to guess. If he has fifty or a hundred staff or more he will have a lot on his mind already.

Or maybe the company you're in is limiting you. Maybe you could do better elsewhere; I'll deal with looking for a new job in Chapter Six.

All of these things are secondary to sorting out your spending. If you want any sort of quality of life, you've got to nail this one. One thing that astounded me when I ran a mortgage brokerage was the correlation between bad health and poor credit. In life assurance and mortgage applications, good health and clear credit went hand in hand and, conversely, poor credit and poor health invariably came together.

Money worries can and do affect your physical and psychological health and need to be dealt with. I know from personal experience the effect stress has, not only on myself, but on friends and peers who have been in similar situations. You can only go so long before money worries start to take a toll on your health.

3

I've Lost My Job

Although it's almost twenty years ago that I was fired, the memory of what it felt like stayed with me for a long time. As school had not really been my thing, to understate it slightly, I went to work straight after my Leaving Cert. I got my first job in a commercial insurance brokers. It was an office junior role and a great opportunity. This was the back end of 1990 and I started on £7,500 per annum, a king's ransom for an eighteen year old who was used to a tenner a week pocket money. Unfortunately, this gave me the funds to head out on the tear seven nights a week; I was like a student with a job. I ended up going to work and being the same person I was in school, which was a messer.

This did not work in the real world. After four months I was brought into the manager's office and given one of the biggest kicks in the arse of my career. I was told I was not good enough and that I was being let go.

This had a profound effect on me.

I had lost a great opportunity. Up until that point, any time things weren't going great, I was told that I was smart but that I would not apply myself. This was the first time someone had said I was not good enough.

The opportunity was gone. I did not treat the job with the respect it deserved. It had come too easily. It was the first job I had applied for, I got it the same week, and human nature being human nature, sometimes we don't appreciate the things we get for free half as much as the ones we have to work hard for. But the bit that hit me really hard was being told I was not good enough. Because I knew I was. I got distracted by too much money, bars, beer, nightclubs and whatever else. And this was Ireland in 1990, well before the Celtic Tiger and just out of the eighties recession. It was a really tough place to get a job. I had just pissed my opportunity away, literally.

I didn't tell anyone I got fired. Not siblings, parents, girlfriend, no one. I hoped I could have a new job in time so no one would know. I told God I would have a different attitude to work if he would give me one more chance. I know some people say there is no such thing as God and it's a random sequence of events, and so on, and quite possibly they're right. But there's nothing like the shit hitting the fan to make you start praying! Put a gun to a man's head and see if he prays to a random sequence of events.

So, no, I wasn't made redundant, and I know getting fired for not being good enough isn't the same thing as being let go from a job you've worked hard at for years.

But they say everything happens for a reason and, more importantly, every action has a reaction. If you've just lost your job, how you react to it is going to determine the next part of your life. Sometimes, the thing you wish for is the last thing in this world you need, and the very last thing you want to happen can become the most formative experience of your life. For me, I look back now at getting fired as a young man as the most positive influence on me and my career.

As it happened, I was really lucky. An opportunity came up in sales in another general insurance broker. I went for it, I got it. (I might have omitted on my CV I was being let go by my current employer!) It's funny how something that at the time feels like the worst thing that could ever happen actually becomes a tipping point that can change your life.

This time, it was going to be different. I changed absolutely everything about my attitude to work. I decided that what was important to me was getting a career. I decided to go about succeeding with as much enthusiasm as I could muster and to work as hard as I possibly could to achieve my goals.

So, the most important part of losing your job is how you react to it and what you do next. That will be the difference when you look back in a few years' time. Will you judge it as a catalyst for something great, or will it be the worst thing that ever happened? Had that old boss of mine kept me on, what kind of a man would I be now? I think I would have kept on cruising.

Now What?

So now you have to ask yourself some questions. Have you ever wanted to try something else and never had the chance? Have you ever wanted to set up by yourself? What are you good at? Are you pretty decent with your hands?

Have you ever wanted to run a small business? Every time there is a change, there is an opportunity. You need to look for the opportunity in this change.

As far as I'm concerned, this recession is far and away the greatest opportunity of our lifetime. It's never been easier to set up a company, rent an office, buy equipment and advertise. Everything from printing to phones to property has become cheap and accessible. Most people can't see it because everyone in the media is saying how terrible everything is. Bad news sells. But there are two ways of looking at how things are at the moment. You can see the negative or you can see the positive. At the moment, as bad as things are, all I can see are opportunities. Warren Buffett says, 'Be fearful when others are greedy and be greedy when others are fearful.' As far as I am concerned this is the time to be greedy. One of the best decisions I made last year was to stop allowing myself to be bombarded with bad news every day. I still keep abreast of the news, but I'll mostly just follow the headlines if at all possible. I used to read two newspapers a day. Now if I read one I'll go straight to the business or sports section. I stopped allowing my mood and attitude to be altered and affected every morning, afternoon and evening with bad news, and the quality of my life improved dramatically. Sometimes, censoring your influences is an option if the influences are all negative. I can't control what is going on in Europe and around the world, but I can make a difference to what is directly under my control, so why allow myself to be influenced negatively by what I can't control? Whether our economy grows by 1 per cent or contracts by 1 per cent has no effect on me on a day-to-day basis, so why allow my happiness and quality of life to be affected by a statistic? If the economy contracts by 1 per cent for two consecutive quarters we are in recession – that is how a recession is defined. If it grows by 1 per cent we are not. I don't care. The recession did not kill my businesses. The banks falling apart did. It's not as though mortgages can disappear again on me and leave me with a company with fuck all to sell. If insurance, food, alcohol and the need to live under a roof or the need for offices disappear like mortgages did, then I'm rightly stuffed but, assuming they don't, I can build my companies right up again regardless of whether we are in recession. I don't need people to be throwing money about to thrive.

This may be completely unrealistic, but if you get a bit of redundancy or you have a little cash to spare and it's in any way possible, get yourself away on holidays. They are really cheap at the moment. Losing your job is a very emotional experience and it pays to take a bit of time away to digest things, put the past to bed and work out the next option.

Could you set up a small business? Maybe doing something you love mightn't earn as much, but could it make you happier? There is nothing like loving your job for great quality of life, and hating your job for terrible quality of life. Is spending more time with family a better option? Even for a year or two? There is a lot more to quality of life than money, and nobody ever looked back on their deathbed and wished they'd spent more time in the office.

Or do you simply want to get back into the working world as quickly as possible? If so, your new job is getting a job. You need to get up and start work at 9 a.m. and finish at 5 p.m. every day until you get a job. Take a lunch break and do all of the things you would normally do, but treat it just as you would any other job. If you put the same effort into getting a job as you would into keeping a normal job, you can't help but find employment sooner rather than later.

Similarly, if you are going to set up by yourself or investigate the possibility of starting your own company, you need to treat it just as you would any other job. You need to be at your desk in the morning, because the opportunity you are looking for will not come looking for you. You need to find it.

There is no harm, either, in doing a day or two of voluntary work. Not only is it worthwhile, but it also means you're staying involved in working and it's great for your confidence. It will also work a treat in an interview and on your CV. It says you did not give up, you adapted.

Far and away the hardest part of this process is the first step. The toughest part of a marathon for me is starting the training in the first place. I'm no runner. I'm six feet three inches, weigh fifteen and a half stone and I'm not particularly fast. Getting myself into a situation where I can run for more than four hours was daunting. The hardest part of writing this book was getting myself to the PC. When I first got the notes from the editor, listing everything I had to do, I had a full day of writing planned. I made myself a cup of tea, sat down at my laptop, read over the notes, then read them again. I pictured the work I had to do, stared at the screen a bit more and then stood up, went over to my bed, fixed the pillows, lay down and slept for the day.

It took me another while to get my head ready for it. But then, once you start, you find your rhythm and you don't want to stop.

I saw this recently in a Mongolian guy who does regular work for me. He helped me build Dax Café Bar. I used to call him 'the fixing god'.

'Can you do this?' I'd ask him.

'Yes,' he'd say. 'I just need some two-by-four, some bonding, a few slabs, and it will be done tomorrow.'

He was made redundant recently after his employer lost a contract. I had a meeting with him and gave him some advice.

'Stop looking for work,' I told him. 'What you need to do is hand out leaflets in Dublin 2 just saying, "Handyman available at €15 per hour". Say you do almost everything from plumbing to carpentry to painting and you'll be inundated with work. When people find a good, honest, reliable handyman, they hold onto him forever, especially in Dublin 2. These Georgian buildings need constant upkeep and repair.'

This was my second time of advising him, and I could see as I said this that he really wasn't keen on taking on the responsibility of finding work himself. It's that intimidating first step again. So I took matters into my own hands. I got him in for a day's work delivering leaflets around Dublin 2 for Dax, which said, 'We now do office deliveries.' I also gave him a different bunch of leaflets: 'Handyman available. Honest, hardworking, €15 per hour, etc., etc.' When he got back that day, Dax had received no calls for takeaways, but he had three jobs.

When I was in Australia in 2001, I was twenty-eight

years old, on holidays and finding it hard to get casual work. The best I could get was about ten dollars an hour, and I had just been let go from a sandwich shop after a day and a half. Apparently, when you're employed on a temporary basis in a sandwich shop, they don't really need your tips on management. So I decided to see what I could do to generate more income. I picked up a bucket and car cleaning equipment and offered to valet people's cars. Okay, it was not the most fabulous work in the world, but I could set up anywhere, work my own hours and make way more money that I could anywhere else.

The point is, you can make money anywhere and anyhow, especially if you are willing to do something that saves people time, money or heartache. It doesn't have to be a great invention. You just have to be prepared to take that first step.

Back in Dublin, the rumours were flying.

'McGuire's gone troppo . . . I heard he's washing cars in Sydney and going to work on a skateboard.'

'I heard he is living in a wigwam in Byron Bay.'

'I heard he is living in a hut on a beach in Thailand.'

It was all true, but I knew what I was doing.

Get Fit

One of the best things you can do when you are taking these steps, whether it's the search for a new job, or research into next directions, or setting up a new company, is getting yourself fit. If you don't do much sport, you have absolutely no idea how being fit makes you look at things differently, especially when taking on a new challenge. Getting to the gym at seven in the morning means you're firing on all cylinders by the time you hit work at nine. I only got fit in my early thirties. I started playing five-a-side to deal with stress, because I could not get work out of my mind when I was trying to sleep. There is nothing like being involved in a sport to make you completely forget about the day you've just had. Now I go to the gym and it puts me in great form and gives me great energy. I just wouldn't have the same attitude without fitness. Nowadays, give me a few weeks without exercise and I'm miserable.

First Things First

Whatever your next move is going to be, there are a number of important practical and urgent things you need to take care of ahead of anything else. First, write to your mortgage provider and request a change to your mortgage until you sort out your entitlements with the social welfare or get a new job. If you have been given a redundancy package, ask to change to interest only.

To work out how changing to interest only reduces your monthly mortgage, just multiply the amount you owe (for example €200,000) by the interest rate (say 2.1 per cent) and divide by twelve for the monthly amount. €200,000 × 2.1% = €4,200.00 divided by 12 = €350 per month.

If you have received no redundancy or if you are not entitled to Jobseeker's Benefit, you will probably need a payment holiday for a couple of months. Going interest only, it should be said, is much better than taking a payment holiday. In the former case, because you are keeping up the interest payments, the amount you owe isn't going up, but with a payment holiday, interest is being added while you're not paying.

But that's a long-term concern. In the short term, balancing your outgoings with your income is the major priority. Be sure to explain to your mortgage provider that you will be back with a full plan as soon as possible. Given their backlog, dealing with social welfare could take quite a while, so your new mortgage arrangement will have to last at least twelve weeks. The hoops you have to jump through will be different depending on the bank. Some will ask for everything and the kitchen sink and make it as awkward as anything. Others will be fair and deal with it quickly and efficiently. Don't let them put you off by asking for a ton and a quarter of paperwork.

There are two types of unemployment benefit. They are now called Jobseeker's Benefit and Jobseeker's Allowance. The latter is means-tested. If you have been paying PRSI for less than two years, you probably won't get the Jobseeker's Benefit. That puts you in the Jobseeker's Allowance category, which means you'll have to be means-tested. If you have been paying PRSI or stamps, you will get Jobseeker's Benefit for between nine and twelve months. You'll also need to apply for a mortgage interest supplement. This is a social welfare payment that will cover most of the interest on your mortgage. There are a range of rules and regulations governing entitlements to this particular support. Contact your local welfare office for full details.

If you're settling into setting up a new business, you need to get back to the bank and request a longer-term interest-only period. Keep it interest only as long as you're setting up or are still on the benefit.

Redundancy Money

What will I do with my redundancy money? There are so many variables here that it is impossible to give broad, sweeping advice. I've simplified it by breaking it down into the major considerations.

Should I Pay Off Part of My Mortgage?

This depends on whether you are on a tracker rate or not. If you are paying 2 per cent on a mortgage and can get 3.5 per cent interest on your lump sum, I would not be so keen. However, with a variable rate, the thinking is completely different. Far more than just the recent increases in the European Central Bank (ECB) rate were passed on by the banks. I expect them to keep on attacking their variable rate customers so, personally, I'm eager to reduce the balance on any of my variable rates. But my trackers I'll keep forever, because it's unlikely we'll see them again in our lifetime. But then again, if a cash lump sum could get rid of your mortgage almost entirely, that's an attractive proposition also. Remember, though, that cash balances are taken into account in assessing the mortgage interest supplement. If you have a large lump sum you won't get it, but if you have a lump sum paid off your mortgage and little cash, you may still get it.

Future Plans

What are your long-term prospects? If you need to set up a business, you will need some capital, so if that's the case, don't use it all and end up going to the bank in six weeks' time for a business loan which you won't get. Hold onto some cash. Also, once you pay money off the mortgage, that's it, it's gone. You won't ever see it again. If you expect to be working on a reduced income and depending on your circumstances, I would look at the short-term debt first and, after that, the mortgage.

Other Loans/Short-Term Debt

Suppose you have a redundancy package of €25,000. You have a €150,000 mortgage costing €750 per month and €25,000 in short-term debt with monthly payments costing €600 (say a car loan and two credit cards). If you use your €25,000 to clear your short-term debt, it reduces your outgoings from €1350 per month to €750 per month, whereas if you pay it off the mortgage, it reduces your monthly outgoings from €1350 to only €1100 approximately. In this instance, I would definitely clear the short-term debt. It makes no sense to clear if off the mortgage. If you have a number of loans, you need to work out which costs the least to clear. For example, let's say you have three loans:

A) A car loan for €9,000 with 12 months left, costing €350 per month;

B) A credit card debt of €4,000 costing €120 per month;

C) A €14,000 credit union loan with five years left costing €250 per month.

If you clear A & B you save €470 per month in outgoings. Clearing the credit union loan takes €1,000 more in cash and only reduces your monthly outgoings by almost half, €250 per month. You need to be smart and have all of this kind of information to hand.

If your plan is to work on a reduced income in something you love, use any cash to bring your monthly outgoings down as much as possible. Car loans and credit cards tend to have the highest monthly outgoings. Be careful who you get advice from on this one. Go to a financial adviser if you need a bit of help, but see if you can get a recommendation from someone good and honest, and don't let them charge too much. Just make sure you don't go to one of your creditor banks looking for advice on who you should pay back. They are not impartial.

Remember, every time there is a change, there is an opportunity. If you have been made redundant, use that change to your benefit, whether it's to generate more family time, to create a new business or even to do voluntary work. If you have a CV with no holes in it because you were doing voluntary work, your attitude will jump off the page. Some of the worst things that ever happened to me turned out to be catalysts for much better times. But you've got to see these disasters in that light, and use them as such.

These are great websites for much more technical information on redundancy and welfare entitlements: *www.itsyourmoney.ie*, *www.welfare.ie*, *www.survivingredundancy.ie*, *www.citizensinformation.ie*.

4

My Job is on the Line

Most people have been hit by reductions in income via the Universal Social Charge and changes to income tax. For those with tracker mortgages, this was balanced somewhat by the reduction in the ECB rate by a whopping 3.5 per cent in the last three years. But for those with variable and fixed rate mortgages, there has been no avenue to recoup any of these losses. To my mind, this is one of the great unnoticed injustices of the past few years. Our insolvent banks need to balance their books, same as any business, and the easiest option for them is to hit their mortgage customers on standard variable rates. It's like shooting fish in a barrel, and I see no sign of it stopping. The banks and the government, being the largest shareholder in them, need to become profitable as soon as possible. So, basically, what we're dealing with here is an inequitable, indirect tax. The banks are losing money and because they're not open for new business, their only mortgage option for generating revenue is their non-tracker rate customers. These customers can't move to another provider, either because there's no refinance available anywhere or because of negative equity (where the mortgage amount is higher

53

than the property value). The variable rate customer has nowhere to go.

So, you can have two families with the same earnings living in the same estate. Both have their mortgages with the same bank but one is on a tracker and one on a standard variable rate. One has the same take-home pay as a few years ago, whereas the other might be on the breadline. So, for some of us, a pay cut is not just unfortunate. It's unaffordable.

How to Take the Cut

A reduction in income or work can come in many different forms: a straightforward pay cut; being asked to accept reduced hours; temporary lay-off, or being put on short-time working. If I was asked to accept a pay cut, the first thing I would establish is whether or not it was necessary. Although it's unlikely in most situations, it's no harm to see if it's just opportunism on the part of the employer. In most cases, it should be glaringly obvious if the company has taken a serious hit as a result of the downturn. If you don't accept the reduced working hours, your employer may make you redundant. Ask yourself, is this a better option for you? In my company there were salary reductions which were accepted because it was obvious the company was losing money. Half the time staff were being paid by personal cheque rather than company cheque. So you can probably see the situation for yourself. Has your company just lost a big contract, or is it obvious that things are slowing right down?

Before you make any decision, make sure you've got full information from your employer. Because he's proposing a change to your contract of employment, you need to agree to the change. Before you agree, you need to find out a few things. Is everyone being treated the same? What are their criteria for picking who will be kept on and who won't? Is what's proposed a temporary measure?

Maybe the thing to do is take some pain temporarily until things improve . . . I use the term 'temporarily' intentionally. If I agreed to a reduction in salary, and I had come to the conclusion that this company and this employer still offered the best option for my future, I would accept the reduction for an agreed time if possible. From an employer's point of view, help from the floor to allow the company to survive should be greatly appreciated and should be rewarded in the long term. But this is a call you have to make yourself.

If possible, agree to a reduction for, say, six to twelve months, with a commitment to review the situation then. If not, I would look for a commitment that if business improved or the company became profitable again, the reduction would be reversed. Once you agree to a reduction, it might be difficult to get it back when things start going well again. You could find that next time you have a meeting about salary, it will be viewed as a raise request as opposed to a reinstatement.

Redundancy

Before you get to that point, you need to thoroughly investigate all of the options. Would negotiating a four-day week be better? How about negotiating a redundancy package and clearing debt or mortgage and starting something new? Most people don't know this but the employer can claim back 60 per cent of a redundancy payment. So, if you are entitled to redundancy of €30,000 (the statutory entitlement is only two weeks' pay per year of employment), it will only cost your employer €12,000, because they can claim back the €18,000. It will take the employer forever and a year to get that money back, but no need to bring that up in a negotiation! So, one option may be to negotiate more than the two weeks per year payment – it's not uncommon to get up to six weeks per year worked, then get out and see what else is about for you.

Your statutory redundancy is tax free. You'll need to check with the tax office or your payroll administrator for info on your tax liability on amounts over and above that. If you're unsure of your current job, or if, long term, there are better or more exciting opportunities out there, a nice tax-free lump sum might not be a bad way to finish up.

There is an exemption for claiming Jobseeker's Benefit after redundancy but it's only for one to nine weeks for amounts between €50,000 and €90,000. So not hugely relevant in my eyes.

I didn't let any staff go over the past few years. I've fired more than my fair share of people for not working hard enough or not following my instructions, but I've never made anyone redundant. I decided I would make sure there were jobs for anyone who stuck with me, but maybe in hindsight I should have given them a cash lump sum and let them find better work. A mortgage company fighting for survival was not the most pleasant place to be.

Reduced Hours

If redundancy isn't an option, a shorter working week may be. If you work only three days per week, you may be entitled to claim Jobseeker's Benefit for the days you spend looking for work. Because a shorter working week could save on travel and childminding, this may be a workable option. I don't want to sound like a gobshite who can only see the good in every situation, but every time there is a change, there is an opportunity. A shorter working week gives you a chance to look for, say, part-time work, or to investigate a whole new area. Do you love your current job, or is it just okay? I know for the past few years I was not doing my job out of love but necessity. In fact, if I had worked in First Credit instead of owning the company, I may have resigned as well! If I had had an opportunity to work in a non-stressed environment, learning the ropes for two or three days a week, that would have sounded very attractive. As it was, I was setting up new businesses and it was these that kept me sane.

Use reduced hours to see what you can make of the opportunity for new work. Is there anything else you have ever wanted to do but never got around to? What are your hobbies? What have you an interest in? Let's say your hobby is DIY or fashion (I'm talking about two different people here). Could you try and get part-time work in a shop or company in that industry? If you have a reduction in hours, and this is the angle you want to pursue, make sure you get a full day or days off rather than a couple of hours here and there, so you can look for and take up other work when you're off.

Can't Afford a Pay Cut?

Suppose you decide after going through all the options that your best alternative remains with your current employer. But you're already underwater, and you just can't afford another pay cut. First of all, you need to do the same spreadsheet I talked about in Chapter One, and go through all of your costs. If a reduction is unaffordable and redundancy is also a non-runner, go have a private chat with your employer and explain that you simply cannot afford the reduction. There are always exceptions to be made. I can't see myself as an employer insisting on a reduction if the employee has gone through their figures with me and simply can't afford it.

If your employer won't back down on a pay cut, you will need to look at income-boosting schemes or negotiating with your creditors as detailed in Chapters One and Two. If you have a family and are on low pay, there are several social welfare schemes that you may be eligible for. The Family Income Supplement gives extra support to families on low pay who have at least one dependent child under eighteen. You may also be entitled to fuel allowance, back-to-school clothing and footwear allowance, or a medical card.

The obvious option in these situations is to quit and find another job, but if you do take up a new position in a new company, the first thing you lose is your right to redundancy from the old one. Even if the company goes bust, you're entitled to a redundancy payment via your social insurance, so if you are in a business field that is in rapid decline, it may well be worth your while waiting to see what happens, and protecting that right to redundancy.

The other important factor is that in Ireland there really is no protection for an employee in the first year of employment. Most contracts set a probation period of six months, but really you don't have any rights until after twelve months. So, if your employer is in a precarious position and you've been working there for less than a year, the wait-and-see option may not be for you. If you've decided to stay, satisfy yourself that your prospective employer is solvent and likely to remain so.

Short-Time Working or Temporary Lay-Off

Short-time working is another way of describing a situation where you are working less than half of your usual hours, or are receiving less than half of your normal pay due to a shortage of work, usually meant to be temporary. If you're working more than half of your usual hours, what you're talking about is a reduction in working hours. If you have been reduced to a three-day working week from five days, that's a reduction in working hours, not short-time working.

Temporary lay-off just does what it says. These are situations where the employer believes that his problems are short term in nature. Remember that you are entitled to know the reasons for the short-time working or the temporary lay-off. The employer is also required to keep you abreast of developments during the time you have reduced work or are laid off. If these measures are not customary in your workplace or in your contract of employment, your employer will need to get your approval. In effect, these options are just alternatives to redundancy. If you feel redundancy is a better option, you should have a chat with your employer (remember, he gets back 60 per cent of the redundancy payment) and discuss your options.

If you're not happy with the short-time working arrangement and wish to be made redundant, but your employer does not want to make you redundant, you can force his hand. You have to give your employer notice in writing that you want to claim redundancy under the Redundancy Payment Acts. To qualify, you must have been on short-time working for four weeks in a row or, if it's broken up, six of the last thirteen weeks. You have to do this within four weeks of short-time working ending. If the employer does not want to make you redundant, he can give counter notice, which means he has to give you thirteen weeks' unbroken employment without lay-off or short time. If you claim redundancy in this fashion you lose your notice period, i.e. the weeks you work after your resignation is handed in. If you are on short-time working or are temporarily laid off, you are entitled to Jobseeker's Benefit or, if you don't have enough PRSI, Jobseeker's Allowance to tide you over. Before you make your move, ring the Citizens Information Board on 021 452 1600 or 1890 777 121 and make sure of your position and entitlements. You can also log onto *www.citizensinformation.ie*. They have local offices around the country, some of which are open until 9 p.m. Remember, the mobile companies fleece you if you ring 1890 numbers, so use a landline if at all possible.

5
My Business Has Folded

First of all, my heart goes out to you. I understand completely how you feel. You hate the idea of anyone knowing your business is gone. You go through a range of emotions trying to make sense of it all.

'My stomach hit the floor.' This expression describes perfectly the feeling I had on an almost daily basis for two years. It perfectly captures the sharp, empty pain that hits you in the midriff and makes you feel like your stomach has dropped out of your body. The only thing I can compare it to is a similar feeling from my teenage years when I was in so much trouble with parents, teachers and pretty much everyone, when there was no escape and no way I could talk my way out of it. I just had to take it on the chin and hope for the best. I forgot all about this feeling through my twenties and early thirties. But it became a regular feature of my late thirties.

I am using this as an example for a reason. It's important to remember that these terrible feelings are all temporary. They are of a particular moment and then they pass. Can you remember when you were a teenager and it honestly looked like there was no way for things to improve? Now remember looking back a few years later and smiling and thinking about how wrong you were, and how you wish you could go back and tell yourself at fifteen that life becomes unrecognizably better? Well, if you are in a situation where your business has folded or is very close to folding, it is really important to remember that this is one of the lows. It will pass. You will get through it. In a while, how you came back from this will be one of your major life stories.

No matter how bad and isolated you feel and how bleak the outlook seems, time and new opportunities and a fresh start will change how you think and feel right now and will set you on a new trajectory. So, the most important thing to recognize is that this will end. When you are down in the dumps, it's important to look around and recognize where it is you actually are. When you're at rock bottom, the only way is up. You need to be strong and let time take care of things.

I'm not out of danger yet; I'm still very much in the fight. But I only have to look back nine or ten months to see rock bottom. My girlfriend said recently that she had forgotten how much of a laugh we used to have. I was losing money for so long it affected who I was. It's hard to be in a good mood when you're slowly watching things disintegrate around you. It's only since I turned it around and became solvent again that we realized what had become the new normal for us. She had forgotten that, really, I'm a messer. Once work is finished, I just want to have a laugh. She had forgotten that, and so had I.

I know other people who were in worse situations than mine, who kept a sunny outlook the whole way through.

I have to admit I really look up to them. It was one of these who pointed out that if he had not had a family, he would have moved into one of his vacant offices, too. I did not need any validation for my decision, but it was good to know there were others who would also take the fight head-on. It's a funny one, watching what you have spent so long building up disintegrating in front of you. It's almost as though you are watching it happen to someone else. I think I made the right call in keeping my company, because I have returned it to profitability now, but maybe the best call would have been to finish it and move on.

Sometimes, your business can be like a bad relationship. You know it's bad for you but you've had such good times and great memories. You've put so much effort into it that it's really difficult to make that call and say, that's it, it's over.

Richard Eberly's Rea Mortgages was the first of my competitors to go. I spoke to Richard a little while ago. He saved himself a lot of pain by going into liquidation early rather than going through the slow, dragged-out death that others had. Sometimes, that's the better thing to do. Say it's over, finish it, take a break and get stuck in again.

Glenroe

I was shocked in October 2008 when, along with many of you, I watched stock markets, pension funds and everything else get annihilated. October 2008 was when the phone stopped ringing in my company, but it was in 2009, when it really hit the fan, that the business world really stopped turning and the cash reserves started to run out.

I didn't sleep much during 2009 or 2010. One mistake I made was not talking about it enough. On one occasion, I remember saying to someone close to me, 'This is the second month I've had to put €35,000 into the company to pay the wages.'

I got a shocked stare. 'Oh my God!'

After that, I decided I'd keep news like that to myself. Back then, in 2009, it all felt temporary. The collapse in everything from stocks to the availability of mortgages felt like a temporary drop, so I decided to fund the company, then take it back when sales figures improved in a few months' time. But that business model was over. The figures did not get better and over the next two years, the company needed constant propping up.

By 2010 things were different. The reality that economic conditions were not temporary but permanent hit home. There would be no mortgages and, as a result, my main business was obsolete. I was no longer worth tens of millions, but about minus four million. I know that's the most attention-grabbing thing on paper but, honestly, I couldn't have cared less about my net worth. The real stress was being involved in so many enterprises and seeing them all get hit at the same time.

My property business is in my own name, and a lot of my business tenants could not afford to pay me because no one was paying them. My residential tenants either left or couldn't afford to pay either. First Credit started losing money every month and I was pouring my own money in just to keep it going. I was investing in Quotedevil and, because it was still at the set-up stage, there was no income coming from that. My buildings on Pembroke Street were vacant for over a year while I was waiting on planning permission for Dax Café Bar, so I was getting no rental income from those. I had a building site in Ballsbridge that was being funded by a mortgage. The bank pulled out of the finance halfway through because they had a clause in the loan offer which said they could. This left me high and dry with a hole in the ground in Ballsbridge worth nothing.

I had €7 million of mortgages on fixed rates of over 5 per cent that I could no longer afford. I had Dax Café Bar yet to build and fund. I had stacks of bills left over from normal trading that would usually be paid out of cashflow, but when a business stops, you are suddenly left with all the usual bills for a company with a turnover ten times what it has become. You're getting calls from the electricity and the gas people telling you that there are overdue bills to be paid and, if they are not paid, you will be cut off. You're trying to work out where you're going to get the money to pay the staff at the end of the month and service all of the outstanding loans. Was this going to be another month where you'd have to blitz your savings?

It always was.

Every month, I'd pore over an Excel spreadsheet. €40,000 and change to go out and no matter how I cut it, about €25,000 and change coming in. I was paying bills as soon as I possibly could but the stack just did not seem like it was diminishing. I had to deal with the sheriff because the Revenue had sent him one of my companies' overdue tax bill. As well as the building site in Ballsbridge which was soaking up money, I was also building Dax Café Bar. I was project-managing the build myself; a full-time stressful job on its own.

I was also chairman of two new companies, while First Credit had shrunk to become a one-man show from eighteen staff two years earlier. So I was answering all the phones, opening the post and doing everything myself, just like when I set up in the first place. And to top it all off, I was living in an office: 200 square feet, with a mattress, a thing from Argos for my clothes, a TV and no kitchen. You nearly want to drill into your brain to relieve the pressure.

Eventually, what felt like the straw that would break the camel's back was when Revenue put an attachment on my account over late payment fees for tax. I was blocked out of my own bank account. The actual tax itself had been paid. They blocked my account over late payment fees. There is just no messing with these guys. When they tell you to pay something, you pay it. Them's the rules, but I really felt like crying at that stage. I just wanted to shout, 'Will you please all just give me a fucking break and leave me alone, I'm doing everything I can. I'm not spending any money on me, I'm just working to pay everyone else.'

Everyone, including banks, wanted everything owed to them, and all at the same time. Overdrafts and loans were being called in. Ask for a loan and it was an automatic 'No'.

'But I've never missed a payment.'

'Yes, but your exposure to us is too high.'

There was no credit for anything. You need it now? You pay now. And all through this time I had a High Court action hanging over me from an architect I had parted company with. It was this one my mum would bring up every time we talked.

'I don't want to talk about it, Mum.' It spent enough time running through my head along with everything else when I was trying to sleep, without my mind giving it more of my time during the day.

Each time something terrible happened, I would look at the extra pressure and know I could not deal with it. But I had to. I'd tell myself, it's okay, it's temporary. But it never was.

What I am probably most happy about is that, despite it all, I didn't have a nervous breakdown and I did not lash out at anyone (though I may have been a pain in the hole).

I used to live for social occasions but, at that time, I had to be coerced into going to anything. The only people I wanted to meet were a very short list of friends and family. Once, I might have been organizing trips to the country, activities and weekends away. Suddenly, the idea of meeting people would put me in a cold sweat. When I was forced into going away, the first day would be tough. It would take a huge effort to speak to people. By the second day, I would be in great form and having great craic and then by Sunday, when it was time to go home, I would be like a child told to go to bed when the house is full of relatives and visitors. I didn't want to go back to the real world. I'd have that Sunday night feeling I used to get when I was younger, brought on by the music to *Glenroe*, when you knew the fun and the weekend were over. Back to the real world and school in the morning, homework still to do and probably in trouble with everyone tomorrow. I swear, when they are lowering me into the ground and I'm on my way to meet my maker, I'll hear the *Glenroe* music ringing in my ears. Da na na na na na na na na na.

Where to Get the Cash?

Anyway, in order to finish the site, build the bar and keep everything going, I needed another million at least. Since I still had hundreds of thousands in outstanding bills, I decided to fire sell everything I could. I sold my cars, my holiday home, my stocks and shares, unit-linked funds, commodities and everything non-property-related that I had spent the past ten years building up. I haven't calculated how much I reinvested to keep things going because it's not an exercise I'd enjoy, but it's into the millions, anyway. Was it the right call? I hope so, but I won't know for a few years. If I'm ever asked in Dax Café Bar, 'Do you still have your Aston Martin?' I answer, 'You're drinking in it.' I eventually got money out of that bank but they did bully me off my tracker to get it. But that's another day's work.

Investing at the same time as losing money is tough. It's bad enough when you're down to your last half a million. When you're down to your last quarter of a million, you're thinking you can still do a legger. Then, before you know it, you're down to your last €100,000, then eventually nil. You've nothing left. Every time, you're second guessing your decision. Am I going to end up with nothing? Am I going to be one more entrepreneur that thought they could trade out of it but couldn't? You keep asking yourself, am I the delusional loser at the blackjack table who won't go until all of his money is gone?

The reality of my situation is that I could have taken an easier ride. The options were there, but really I did not fancy them. I don't like backing down from a fight. I could have let out the ground floor instead of building Dax Café Bar with my business partner Olivier. I could have left the building site until a better time. I could have allowed First Credit to become a non-trading business for a few years and gone to live abroad. I guess there was a certain amount of ego involved in these decisions. My attitude was, I'll take this on. I'll fight you. Ego might be considered a bad word, but where would we be without ego? I wouldn't have forty-odd employees. I'd be bored but comfortable abroad.

I get a bit emotional writing this, because I have to put myself back where I was when it was happening. Nine months later and only now am I getting out of that frame of mind and getting back to being myself. This kind of stress takes time to work its way out of you. Recently, I had to go through bank statements from 2009 and 2010, and that brought me right back there. 'DR' on every balance and referral fees all over the place.

October 2010 was the worst.

I'd used all of my cash and all of my investments to keep everything afloat. I had just built a property that cost millions, I'd built Dax Café Bar without finance from a bank, I had losses in the hundreds of thousands of euros in my companies and was completely out of cash (more than out of cash, actually). I needed new sources of income because I could no longer afford to fund my loan repayments.

If I didn't get the property I had just built in Ballsbridge rented, if Dax Café Bar didn't start trading profitably, if Quotedevil.ie didn't start standing on its own, it was all over. If any one of these failed, I was into arrears and back in the same situation I was two years earlier. Everything I had done for the previous two years would have been for nothing. I was out of options. There was nothing more I could do. Either it was going to work or it was over.

Then, within the space of two weeks, everything started falling into place. I got the building site finished and rented to a good tenant for a decent income. Olivier and I opened the bar. Once it was built, I handed it over to him. He's the brains behind the food and wine; I'm the commercial side.

'Okay,' I said, 'it's your turn, I'm finished. I've been breaking my back carrying this around for nine months, it's your turn to show it some love.'

I went into the bar for lunch the first day we opened and there was a miserable crowd in. That was an atrocious feeling. I was thinking to myself, 'Well done, you genius.'

I went back the next day, nervously anticipating the same kind of numbers. The place was rammed. I could not believe my eyes. I had to leave because I couldn't get a seat. Then Quotedevil.ie made its first monthly profit at almost exactly the same time. Two major projects were finished. I could take a backseat and just concentrate on my day job.

Once I got over the initial elation, which lasted a few days, the reality that I could stop fighting took over. I experienced a huge rush of emotion. I'll admit I had tears in my eyes. I had just moved out of the office and into a great pad. Not as good as pre-recession days, but a pretty decent pad in the city with a kitchen and a bedroom – walk-in wardrobe and all!

Just at the very last minute, when I was out of cash, out of time and out of options, everything started earning. Everything started ticking over. I could stop. I could finally stop and think about it all, because up to that point, I hadn't let myself think about it in case I didn't want to keep going.

I ended up having a few drinks by myself, trying to come to terms with it. What the fuck just happened? Did everything go? Why aren't you in your house? Where's your car? Where's all of your money? I had a weekend of feeling sorry for myself. I came so close to the wire. I was so lucky to have come out of it. But those monkeys take a long time to shake off your back.

Crazy Laws

The grass is always greener on the other side. Every so often, I think maybe I shouldn't have put in that effort to stop the company going bust, but if I hadn't, I sure as hell would be sitting here regretting not putting more of an effort in to keep it going. So, whatever side of this you're on, regrets happen. They do nothing except slow you down. What's the point? It's all about what you learn from these things. Whatever side we come out on, we're probably more rounded people, but we're definitely better business people. One or two bad decisions do not make you a bad business person. For a lot of us, what actually happened was that the raw materials we needed to function were taken away. In my circumstance, I was selling mortgages. It was the equivalent of being a publican and prohibition being brought in. What do you do then? You try and sell orange and Coke, but the demand isn't the same and you still have your premises and staff and outgoings. Although mortgages are not banned completely, as the banks have no funds they make it so difficult and heartbreaking. Getting a mortgage through in Ireland is like pushing a stubborn donkey up a wet hill.

Why are we, as a country, so slow at implementing changes when what needs to be done is glaringly obvious to everyone? The Criminal Assets Bureau is an astounding success, but for years before it was established, criminals could display extravagant wealth without fear of conviction, and even pay tax on their criminal earnings without proving where it came from. It was obvious to everyone that it had to be tackled. Why did it take the murder of Veronica Guerin for these changes to be made?

How many people in the past two years have taken their own lives because of our antiquated bankruptcy laws? How many lives would have been saved if we had had something like Chapter Eleven in the USA? Or even something like they have in the UK, where you can be back after bankruptcy in twelve months? Yes, there is legislation due this year, but why isn't it already in place? I have absolutely no doubt that if we had had proper legislation to deal with what's happened and a different attitude to business failure, less lives would have been lost. If you have to declare bankruptcy, it's game over for you. Why do you have to wait twelve years to start again? Surely, that's wrong from every viewpoint.

The most awful part of this system is how individuals can use limited companies to repeatedly shaft people and other companies without any fear of conviction. This has been going on for years, especially in the building industry, and it needs to be completely overhauled.

The way some people use limited companies is, in my mind, stealing. In the building world they're called 'Subby

Busters'. Builders use limited companies to set up, then they're closed down owing huge amounts to subcontractors, who are instantly put out of business, hence the term 'Subby Buster'. This is not limited to building companies, either. But the way it works in this country, a lot of the time it is up to the victim to pursue and prove reckless trading. It's very difficult and very costly to try and prove that it was a business person's intention to shaft. Set that against our crazy bankruptcy laws, where you have legitimate, honest business people almost tarred and feathered for twelve years.

Trouble Up North

I know this situation well because, about five years ago, an individual used a company to try and steal from me. I invested in a company up north that had pitched a website and algorithm to me that they had developed and which, at the time, I thought looked like a sound investment. It was a Business Expansion Scheme (BES), which means you get a tax refund on your investment. If you invest €20,000, it might only cost you €10,000. It was at the end of the year and there was a deadline, and I didn't do as much research as I normally would.

So I invested in this company. A few months later, I wanted to find out how things were going, so I rang the guy, got his message minder, left a message but didn't get a call back. I rang again, and again and again, then I emailed, then called again and again. This continued for a year or two. I can't remember exactly how long. What I can remember is not having my €20K and not getting any calls or emails back. What I can remember is that horrible feeling of having been ripped off.

I got onto Revenue and, of course, they had received no details of my BES investment. So nothing had been done. He had taken my money and, well, that's it really. He had taken my money full-stop. So I looked up his presentation and got details about his company, then rang as many people and companies as I could to see what I could find out. I wish I had done all of this before I put the money in, but here again is another valuable lesson. Basically, I was told that he had done the same to business people all over the north. He had basically used his company to steal. I also spoke to the gardaí, who told me that it was going to be almost impossible to prove there was anything criminal in what this guy did. They referred me to the Office of the Director of Corporate Enforcement and I was told that I'd have to be able to prove reckless trading. But I could while away my life trying to make that stick, and what would the cost be? €50,000 in the High Court? How do I go about proving there was reckless trading if I can't even get anyone to take my calls? How do I prove to the gardaí that it was criminal?

The whole system is a sham. I read recently that Jim Lacey was barred from being a company director because of gross negligence when he was chief executive of National Irish Bank. Fifteen years ago! I was a kid when that story broke. Nothing has been done with anyone in Anglo Irish Bank except for an attempted perp walk for Seanie Fitzpatrick. If this was America the whole thing would be finished now and there would be a lot of people behind bars.

How can it be possible for someone to get away with using a company to rip people and companies off for hundreds of thousands of euros? And, at the same time, you can get a criminal conviction for pilfering a Mars bar from a Spar. How is this right?

Anyway, I realized I needed to sort this out myself. In talking to other companies up north, I found out that he had opened a shop in a certain border town. Armed only with a bag of leaflets and a sign, I got a flight to Derry Airport, hired a car and went out west to look for this shop. I found it without too much difficulty. I went in and there he was.

'Do you remember me?'

'Yes, John.'

'Is there somewhere we can talk?'

We went into his office and I explained exactly where I was with him. 'I am here for my money. I know how many people you owe money to. I don't care what you say to me now. I have a six-foot sign which says: "the ------ rip off" and a bag full of leaflets explaining exactly what you did. If I don't leave with my money now, I'm staying outside your door telling everyone what you have done to me and to so many others until I get my money or you are out of business.'

There was a five-second gap. 'Is Sterling okay?'

I then spent about twenty nervous minutes waiting for him to come back in. If ever there was a time I questioned myself, it was then. I was afraid four lads with baseball bats were going to show up . . . Anyway, he came back after twenty minutes with £15,000 in cash. Compared to a twenty-euro note, a twenty-pound-Sterling note is physically a way bigger note: £15,000 is a really substantial block of cash. So here I was, stuffing wads of twenty-pound notes into my jacket pockets, my jeans, my inside pockets . . . anywhere I could find a space. Then I started thinking, 'Hang on, you're on your own up here, where you know no one, with £15,000 in used twenties stuffed everywhere. What are you doing?' Then I did actually get really nervous. Get to a bloody bank quick! I was worried about being followed, so I got into my £29 rental, which was a little Peugeot with a 1.9cc turbo diesel engine. I raced back into Derry, saw a First Trust bank, went to the cashier and asked for a bank draft. I don't know what I was thinking. I own a financial services company, I know money-laundering procedure. You can't just go into a bank with twenties sticking out of everywhere and get a draft! How could I have been so stupid? The cashier looked at me as though I was nuts. 'Sir, you can't just get a bank draft for cash without having a bank account here. You need to go to your own bank.'

So I found out there was a branch of my own bank in Letterkenny. I raced there and walked in like the Michelin man and started taking the wads of cash out of my clothes to lodge in my account. Ordeal over.

But the point here is, no one else who invested in him got their money back. And many of them were owed way more than me. I always try and avoid doing business with anyone who I think would say, 'It's not personal, it's just business.' Business is always personal. People who are prepared to rip you off or shaft you do not have any morals.

It won't keep them awake at night. Embarrassment, though, does seem to work.

Next Steps

Before you make your next move, there is some very important thinking to be done. You have to work out whether you have the correct skill set, aptitude and attitude for business. You need to work out whether it is for you. Would another business end the same way, or would you be better able to deal with the same set of circumstances if they arose again? Have you learnt from what's happened? What caused the end? Was it avoidable? Would you have a greater chance of making a difference in another walk of life? And, most importantly, do you have the hunger to do it again, except better this time?

If you have the time and the resources to take a bit of time off to digest what has gone on, this will give a bit of clarity and maybe grow the hunger again. The reality for most, though, is that it's not possible. If it isn't, you've still got to ask yourself if you would be better suited to a guaranteed pay cheque at the end of each month.

If you do have gaps in your skill set, but you still want to go into business, another option is to go into business with someone who has the skills you lack. It's a tough call which only you can make. Don't be too hard on yourself, and don't let fear of failure be the deciding factor. Many great people have fallen before you. An honest assessment of your abilities is what you need, to help you decide what to do next.

Social Welfare

The social welfare situation is a lot more precarious for those who are self-employed and whose business has folded. Unless you became self-employed in the last two years, you are most likely not in a position to claim Jobseeker's Benefit. If you are not entitled to Jobseeker's Benefit, you may be entitled to means-tested Jobseeker's Allowance. You may also be entitled to unemployment credits or to pay voluntary contributions to help maintain your social insurance record. Help is available if you remain self-employed but are not making ends meet – for example, if you're working as a carpenter but getting very little work. You may also be entitled to help with your mortgage or rent. If you find yourself in this position, the first person you need to talk to is your community welfare officer. Make an appointment with them immediately and get them to help you work out your entitlements.

Having Balls

Being a business owner means that a few bad days at work can finish you. As an employee, a few bad days generally can't. Don't forget you are one of a select few who have had the balls to take the risk and set up their own business. The reason it is intimidating and the reason most people will never experience the highs and lows associated with owning a business is because it takes a certain kind of person.

The kind of person who, regardless of the outcome, decided against the security of a salary and decided, instead, to opt for the potential financial and personal gains that come from setting up a business. I read a report from the UK many years ago that said that successful company directors in the UK had on average two failed businesses behind them. That means that it was third time lucky for most successful directors in the UK. I would say, in the past few years the boom we enjoyed put that statistic way out of date. It's probably more relevant to the economic conditions we are in now, when it's more like the eighties than the nineties. So do not despair. You are in exalted company!

The list of those who have been declared bankrupt or who failed at business, then went on to change the world or achieve great individual success, is seriously surprising. Did you know that Donald Trump was declared bankrupt in 1990? Or that before he set up Walt Disney Animation, Uncle Walt was also bankrupt? Also, Mark Twain, Henry Heinz and Henry Ford. And, most surprisingly, Abraham Lincoln and two other American Presidents have been declared bankrupt. In America, bankruptcy is nearly a rite of passage. I guess what I am saying is, it happens to the best of us. A lot of the people who have shaped the world we live in have been bankrupt, then picked themselves up and kept going until they were successful.

My belief is that it's not how you deal with the good stuff that makes you a successful person. Dealing with the good stuff is easy. Rather, it's how you deal with things when the chips are down. What brings success in most people is the dogged attitude that makes you get back up on your feet and look for another battle after getting the crap beaten out of you. Success is down to the attitude that won't give up. People who consider themselves unlucky often say that success is all about random luck. I do believe in luck, but the harder I work, the luckier I get. The quicker you get on with life and get over the bad luck, the sooner good luck comes and finds you. Success can just be down to who hangs on the longest. But you have to be out there looking for it. Good luck does not find you if you're sitting at home watching *Neighbours* at lunchtime on a Tuesday.

6

I Need a New Job

A parcel landed on my desk a few months ago. It was a curriculum vitae from a chap living in the UK. It was packed with references and letters of congratulations from employers and customers going back years. It also had a very engaging covering letter about how he had fallen in love with an Irish girl and was looking to relocate. There were hand-written notes saying, 'This is the nicest and best CV you will receive this year,' and more. I looked at his letter, CV and all of his brilliant references and thought, this guy is either mad or brilliant. Luckily for him, I don't mind a bit of the crazy; a bit of the crazy can be great (too much is bad!).

So, even though I had no position available, I rang him and organized a meeting. A week later he got a flight over from London and I interviewed him in my offices in Dublin. Through the course of the meeting, he went through all of the areas he thought he could help me with: marketing, PR and sales. He pitched various ideas he had for all of my companies, and he explained at length how he could add value. I offered him a job the next day – a job that did not exist before his letter. He started work for me three weeks later.

My point here is that the first thing you need to make

yourself stand out from the crowd is a killer CV and covering letter. Sometimes, we have a tendency to look at ourselves and think, 'Well, I couldn't have a killer CV because I don't have X, Y or Z.'

Not true. You can make almost anyone look good on paper. This is where you need to work out your strengths and PR yourself. I created a job because of the attitude shown and the way his CV jumped off my desk. I could see from his letter and I understood from his interview that he had marketing acumen. The degree he did or did not have was secondary.

Your CV is your brochure. Think of the effort companies go to with their brochures, and the crap they can make sound good. You have a better product, you just have to work out your selling points. Spend a bit of time researching how to put together a great CV. I worked on a CV for a friend a few years ago. I kept the basic information he gave me but, by the time I was finished, he looked so good on paper that even I wanted to hire him. Remember, this is your pitch on paper, so spend time on it. Tailor it to the specific job you are applying for. What are your best points? Maybe bullet-point them at the start of the CV and highlight them. Make this the focal point of your CV. When I was applying for positions years ago, I did not look good on paper. I had no degree, limited experience and a not-so-great Leaving Cert. With a bit of effort, I still managed to look good on paper by emphasizing my strong points. In large bold, I talked about my sales ability, my work ethic, my ambition, my drive, and so on, together with all of the positives that would benefit the company I was applying to. Had I written it like a normal CV, it would not have read very well at all.

Don't lie. But be smart. I interviewed a guy years ago and in his Leaving Cert section, he put down four honours and three passes. I decided to do a random check and asked to see his results. He had four honours, two passes and a fail. In lying, he managed to manoeuvre himself out of being hired. Had he been smart and said he had four honours and two passes and just left out the fail he may have got the job. There is a huge difference between a lie and spin.

Try and keep your CV to two pages if at all possible. I realize, though, that for some professions this is not at all possible.

Almost every CV I get now is by email. Do yours differently. Do up your CV in a perfectly presented folder and send it in by post. No one else is doing that.

The Approach

How is it that since the recession started, I get less CVs directly than I did when the economy was booming? Surely it should be the other way around. As an employer, suppose you have two CVs and two almost identical candidates, but one has applied to you directly and the other has come through a recruitment company. Since you have to pay the recruiter €5,000 or €6,000, the cheaper option tends to win out, especially in this climate. Look at it like this: the upfront costs of hiring someone are the hardware, software, advertising, training and incidentals. Let's say in total it equals a €10,000 gamble. When there's a recruiter's fee, it's now a €15,000 gamble. So when I am doing the maths on a potential job, I'm just that bit more inclined to go for someone who has applied directly. You are also more likely to take a risk on creating a position when the upfront cost is substantially less and therefore the risk is a lot lower. For example, I have just seen a good CV and am thinking about creating a new sales role for one of my companies as a result. Believe it or not, this happens a lot more than you would think. We will create a job for someone who we don't want to see go to the competition.

Why not call in to the company and ask to speak to the person in charge? Why not hand-deliver your CV? You could even tell a white lie and say you have a meeting. All of these things take effort, work and some balls, but all of them separate you from the crowd. And, by the way, follow-up calls work. Always follow up with a phone call, but not too many, otherwise you look manic!

When I returned from Australia in 2001, I wanted to do one of two things. Either set up by myself again or learn from someone brilliant in a completely new field. At this stage, I had spent a year and a half without a proper job. I had the hunger to learn or to create or to build something new. I also missed taxing my brain.

I took out an advert in the classified section of the *Sunday Business Post*. I was looking for a position in a completely new field with an equity stake and the option to buy out the whole business in a few years' time. It was a simple enough advert saying something along the lines of 'Energetic young businessman with capital and background in insurance and finance seeks to buy a percentage of an existing business with a view to full buyout. May suit someone close to retirement.' Not only did people with companies for sale get in contact, but within a week I had three or four job offers. I had been self-employed since the age of twenty-two, so if there is an opposite to institutionalized, that was me. My default position is to set up my own company, but I do remember thinking that if that didn't work out, this would be the way to get yourself a decent position.

There are two ways of approaching the search for a new job. Wait for it to come to you or go looking for it. Nearly everyone else is waiting for it to come to them. There are always ways to create positions, leads or revenue in recessionary times. If you are unemployed at the moment, why not try and create a job for yourself?

Is there an area of business or a trade or a company that you would love to get into? What are the stumbling blocks? Is it difficult to get into? Are there no vacancies in the company you want to work for? Or do you really need experience to get into it?

National Internship Scheme

Here's a great way to create a job for yourself. There's a scheme called the National Internship Scheme, which has been running since July 2011 and is set to run for two years. This scheme is designed to create jobs in new areas. If a position is created for someone getting a jobseeker's payment or signing for credits, it costs the employer absolutely nothing because wages are paid by the state in the form of social welfare, with a top-up of €50 per week for a period of up to nine months.

To qualify, the company or organization must not have any positions already available. So far, there's been a low take-up on this scheme; it's not known by many employers. So if there is an area of business or a company you want to get into or can't break into because of the downturn, why not find the decision-maker and write a letter detailing, in a way that really stands out, how you can work for them for free under the National Internship Scheme. All they have to do is register. Tell them you will even take care of the paperwork if they want. Tell them the only request you have is that it be in a position where you will learn as much as possible because your objective would be to work as hard as possible to make yourself invaluable over the nine months. If it was at all possible, I would create a job for someone who took that kind of initiative.

'Taking the initiative' is one of these standard interview answers that people rattle off. 'I work well under pressure,' 'I can work off my own initiative . . .' I tend to ignore all of these standard learned lines. But if I got a CV in from someone who made this kind of offer, they have already proven they can work off their own initiative. Once you have made yourself an asset to a company, you can ask to be put on a salary.

Employer Job (PRSI) Incentive Scheme

Then there's the Employer Job (PRSI) Incentive Scheme, where the employer pays only half of the standard employer's PRSI rate for people earning up to €356 per week.

If I was looking to make the jump to a salary, this would be my negotiating tool. If you are put on minimum wage, it's not costing your employer the extra 10.75 per cent PRSI they have to pay for better-paid staff. Someone on €500 per week is costing €553.75. But if you ask for the €356 per week, you're only costing the employer €371.13. This reduced rate of PRSI is only there until January 2014, after which it will be doubled again to 8.5 per cent, so now is the time to take advantage of it.

This Employer Job (PRSI) Incentive Scheme is, therefore, another way of selling yourself to an employer. You could write a letter spelling out how you want to work for the company, offering to work for the minimum wage until you prove yourself. Because of the reduced PRSI Scheme, the cost to the employer of employing you is at its lowest in years. Selling yourself like this makes the prospect of creating a position far more attractive.

Social Media

Social media sites are a great way of showing your best side to an employer. Also, of course, your worst side because, yes, bosses check social media pages. A few years ago, one of my staff hired an office junior. This junior was the first guy that he hired, so he felt he had a lot riding on him. After only two weeks, he rang in sick with a terrible coughy voice. The poor fella. So we had a quick look on his Bebo page: 'Had a mad one last night so called in sick. The missus is up for the weekend so going to chill out here for the day.'

I wanted to fire him on Bebo: 'Hi, it's your boss here. Great you had a mad one. You're fired.'

But the guy who hired him was so annoyed he made him come in that day just to send him home.

I feel slightly strange talking about social media because I'm a Luddite. Technology isn't my thing, but by using LinkedIn, you have a perfect opportunity to connect with individuals and decision-makers, either in companies or industries you want to get into. It is also a way for employers to check you out. LinkedIn is your personal CV on view. It's your shop window, it's the way you let the industry know you are there, so use it accordingly.

Networking

Although online is a great way of getting connected, face to face is the one that works best for me. I used to hate the idea of networking, the idea of a whole load of people only talking to each other to get something out of it, but the truth is I didn't really understand how it can work. Networking is just meeting people. If you like having a chat, networking is a great way of meeting people and doing business. Just after I set up First Credit I was at a party and someone told me about a group of business people who met at six-thirty in the morning every week to generate business for each other. I thought this sounded fantastic. I was only open a month, so at this stage I would have roller-skated naked down Grafton Street for some revenue. I had no problem getting up at 6 a.m. and, as it turned out, it may have been one of my best moves ever. Not only because I started getting business from it but, more importantly, I met people of my ilk; people who had decided to go it alone and who, like me, were in completely uncharted territory. None of my friends or acquaintances were going in this direction. Other than my dad, I had no one to use as a sounding board. Although I had been self-employed, that was just me working by myself. I had very little experience of building up a company or the growing pains that accompany it. Where do I start trying to sort out hiring staff? Contracts? Wages? What do I know about managing people, about employment law, design, marketing, and so on? How do I go about making a website? Networking introduced me to people who could help me with all of these things. But also, I had people I could call and chat to about how to deal with the day-to-day problems I'd never encountered before.

I ended up doing this kind of structured business networking every week for five years or more. It worked on a quid-pro-quo basis where everyone was generating business for each other. I was sort of afraid to give it up in the end. I was afraid that if I stopped doing all of the small things that made me successful, the big stuff would fall apart.

In addition to getting great business and making great friends out of networking, I also used it to recruit. There was a guy, employed by another company, who used to handle all of my insurance. At the time, he used to make the effort to get up for a meeting with me every week. I approached him after a few years and told him I wanted to set up a commercial insurance brokerage and wanted him to come in with me. We set up Pembroke Insurances in 2005 with him as Managing Director and me as Chairman. Pembroke now has a turnover of circa €3.5 million and is worth a seven-figure sum.

I've said it before, but it's when you are out and about meeting people that opportunities come up. My best networking venue is Dax Café Bar. I've found, too, that when you're in a venue, whatever that venue might be, you never know what kind of synergies a quick chat can unearth. I opened Dax to replace my boardroom, but I've done far more business just randomly meeting people in the bar than I ever did when it was a boardroom. I like meeting people, and it's only when something pops up in conversation that it suddenly becomes networking. Up until then, for me, it's just having a laugh.

Don't do what some people do; don't go straight in for the kill without any small talk. Chat first. Every so often you do meet people who are straight in with the business card. It's like a race to talk to as many people as possible for as short a time as possible just to get the business card in. That, for me, is the card that goes straight into the bin. You can smell the insincerity off them. People do business with people they like. They hire people they like. You only get one chance to make a first impression and most people decide within the first sixty seconds whether they like someone or not. Once my gut tells me something, it's almost impossible to change it. Almost every time I've gone against my gut, I've made a mistake.

I have been wrong occasionally, but if someone does not make a good impression and it is sitting uneasily with me, will I be prepared to take a chance on them? Probably not. Even if there are five interviews and psychometric testing, it's still an individual who decides whether they want to put their name to hiring you or not.

The Interview

When it comes to interview time, remember that appearance makes up so much of that first impression, so make sure you look absolutely immaculate. If you appear in any way scruffy, that is a reflection of who you are and how you will work. I have made up my mind immediately on seeing a candidate whose appearance was not up to scratch. I've cancelled interviews before they started and I've interviewed for less than a minute. If you turn up looking like you slept in a bush last night, what are you going to look like on a Monday morning in four years' time? I'm not going to waste my time going through the motions asking questions when I know I won't hire.

Buy a suit for interviews only. For both men and women, a business suit says you mean business. You don't have to spend a fortune to look great going into an interview, but if you're just starting off, the suit is essential. You can pick one up for less than €200 if you're a guy and around €300 if you're a girl. Make sure it fits properly. If you get a hand-me-down, bring it to a clothes alteration centre and get it taken in to fit you. This will cost no more than €40 or €50. You can see the school leavers each year going for their first jobs or first interviews in suits they are swimming in. We've all been there. I wore my dad's suit until I got my first pay packet. Buy a new white shirt for interviews. You can get a crisp white shirt for €28 nowadays and it will make a suit look really sharp. Nothing's worse than a slightly grey, old white shirt that looks like your cleanest dirty shirt. NEVER leave your top button open. ALWAYS make sure your tie is fully done up. A partially tied tie gives off the worst signal. Learn how to do a Windsor knot. I called into Louis Copeland's shop one afternoon to get taught how to tie a Windsor knot. One of my current best salesmen nearly did not get the job because he had his top button undone and the tie an inch away from his collar. And he had stubble. But my business partner had interviewed him for twenty minutes before I came in and he was very positive about him.

There is no such thing as designer stubble when you're going for a job interview. There are two looks. Clean-shaven and employed, or stubbly and unemployed.

Polish your shoes. Get polish, a shoe brush, cover them in polish and then buff them. With a decent-fitting suit, a crisp white shirt and polished shoes you are making a statement the moment you arrive.

How do you project yourself? The first time you meet someone, smile. It is impossible for them not to smile back. It's almost impossible not to like someone who is smiling, who is happy to meet you. Try it on your enemies. Nothing annoys them as much as a big handshake and a smile. Regardless of how you feel, you need to be friendly and positive. When you're answering questions, make a concerted effort to be in a good mood. If all of these things sound in some way familiar, it's probably because your mother told you before and you ignored her because she was old and out of touch. Next time you're talking to her, tell her she was right.

One of the things I mastered early on in life was hiding my nerves. Everyone gets them. It's what you do with them that counts. Nerves and adrenaline can be used to your advantage. Your brain works quicker when there's adrenaline around. If you feel nervous and uncomfortable and then allow how you feel on the inside to dictate how you look on the outside, you will look miserable. Don't allow yourself to feel anything other than positive and, after a while, even though you have forced it, that feeling takes over. It's no longer forced but natural. The most important feeling an interviewer wants is to like you! He is probably going to have to work with you, so if he likes you, you are more than halfway there.

Being completely honest, there is something I distrust in people who don't know how to shake hands properly. How can you get to this age without finding out that no one likes to hold something that feels like a dead fish? Shake hands like a man. Even if you're a girl. Nothing feels worse than being given a damp, limp hand to hold. Even if it's a dry, limp hand, it's still gross. The worst way to start an interview is to make the interviewer hold a hand that feels like it was left overnight in a stew. If there isn't a tiny wrestle for control in a handshake, you're doing it wrong.

So, now you've got to the interview. Your first impression is in the bag and you look a million dollars. You now need to separate yourself from everyone else who is going for the position. One of the first things you need to have done is what investors call 'due diligence'. This is the process by which they investigate a company they're interested in buying or investing in. You need to have found out as much as you possibly can about your potential employer. Go back as far as you can, try to speak to as many people in that industry as you can. Find out about their people, their expansion history, their offices . . . everything. With Google you have such easy access to information that if you only have a quick look on the company website, you're going to look lazy.

After you've done all of this work, it's your job to PR yourself. Make sure you let the interviewer know how much you've prepared. Don't be afraid to answer a question with an answer that shows the level of research you've done, even if it's not entirely the answer they were looking for. One of the things they teach you on media courses is how to convey the points you need to get across, even if the conversation is going away from you. Have a list of questions or items you want to cover written down before you go into an interview and challenge yourself to get those points across, whatever they may be. Analyse yourself afterwards. Did you get to say everything you wanted to say? Make sure the questions you ask show that you have done the research. There is no point in working hard on something if you don't let the decision-maker know about it. If you are able to ask questions about the company's history, especially if it's information that's not readily available, it will show you are hungry for the job. Years ago, I used to go to the ILAC Library to get information on anyone I was being interviewed by. My main purpose was to demonstrate in the interview that I took time off to do research, regardless of what I found out, and believe me it worked. Take the time to do more than the other interviewees, who are your competitors.

If the position allows it, having something prepared which showcases your thoughts or research is another great idea. It's not appropriate to every position but it really has the potential to jump you a level or two above your competitors. Only recently, I advertised for a marketing manager for one of my companies. At the interview, after a few questions, the candidate said he had done some work and asked if he could show it to me. He produced a fifteen-page PowerPoint presentation on growth areas, prospective business targets, types of marketing, and so on ... More than anything this showed that he is the type to put in hard work and that the position meant enough to him that he had spent hours researching and preparing for the interview. In doing this, he had taken the interview by the scruff of the neck and made it his own. He started work that week.

The good times made both employers and employees sloppy. Revenue was easier to get and laziness crept in everywhere. From an employer's point of view, replacing staff became increasingly difficult and expensive, and it may have been simpler to allow people to get away with more than usual. Average employees had great options because they could walk into other positions. Employers had to raise salaries to recruit and retain staff. Employers may also have taken on staff who, in a harder market, would not have landed the job. Put simply, the bar is lowered during boom times. I am not saying it was a seismic reduction in standards, but they went down far enough for a lot of people born in the late eighties and early nineties not to have any real clue about how to sell themselves in an interview, because they never really needed to.

I, personally, prefer a tougher climate, where everyone is

more honest, in work ethic and attitude. People appreciate their jobs and work accordingly. I would prefer it if things were a little easier for everyone than they are right now, but somewhere between the boom and the current climate is perfect. The real test for all of us, from the bottom to the top, is surviving this and thriving again.

7

I Need a New Career

My younger brother rang me on his mobile from the summit of Mount Kilimanjaro, which he climbed to raise funds for Crumlin children's hospital. I had to walk outside to hear him because I can't get reception in my kitchen. Go figure.

His question was, 'Am I just having a brain fart or am I right in thinking I can do something better with my life?' We had a long conversation that centred on how sometimes change is exactly what's needed, how it can often turn out to be the best move of your life. He came home and did a total career U-turn. Now, as I write this, he is completely bedded into his new career working for a charity. His old career is a distant, bad memory.

I think that sometimes you can have amazing clarity of thought after enormous physical exercise or after achieving a worthwhile target. There are loads of examples of people who have been years down a particular career route but have made the best decision of their lives by changing direction completely.

One of the things this recession has taught us is that it is not all about the money. When the money is gone, what's left? Is there any love there for the job? Or was money the only motivating factor? Before I started writing this, my central idea on changing career during a recession was that it is more risky, because bouncing back into a job if it doesn't work out is far more difficult than it used to be. But having spoken to a few people on this subject, the key thing seems to be that the recession has forced so many of us into analysing ourselves. It's been a huge catalyst for change. Yes, you may not be able to walk straight back into the role that you used to occupy, but isn't that a greater motivation to succeed in the new direction? Knowing that it won't be easy if you fail? Wasn't it the Romans who used to burn the boats of their warriors as soon as they went ashore in an enemy country? There would be no chance of even thinking about giving up.

Til Death Do You Part

Once upon a time, the all-important decision on what you wanted to do for the rest of your life was made at seventeen years of age, and if you got it wrong, you were stuck. How are you supposed to pick a career path that lasts thirty-five or forty years when you're seventeen years old? I couldn't. Some people get it right, but just because you didn't, does not mean you have to stick with it until death do you part. Many people nowadays can have two or three careers in their lifetime, because what suits you at twenty-five may be a world away from what you want at age forty.

When you dislike something which is such an integral

part of your life, you won't always acknowledge how you really feel about it. It's only after you make the decision to leave and really allow yourself to think about it that you wonder why on earth you stayed there for as long as you did. Someone said to me a few years ago that when you find a career you love, you don't work a day in your life. This is so true. When you're really enjoying your job, the day absolutely flies. When you don't, you keep watching the clock. You look up after an hour and the big hand has only moved ten minutes.

We spend more time at work than we do at anything other than sleeping. If you don't enjoy it, you have to do something about it. You've only one life. You can't waste half of it doing something you don't care about.

Taking that jump from one career to another, especially later in life, is difficult, but as with everything in this world, the most rewarding things are always the difficult ones. Nothing compares with that feeling of elation you get when you've achieved something you've worked hard for, be it an exam result, a promotion, a new job or a physical challenge. The elation that comes from taking a risk and seeing it pay off only happens when you try something with no guarantees of success. It comes from going into something thinking, 'I'm really not sure I can do this, I hope I don't regret this.' It's all about not being held back by the possibility of regret. If it wasn't difficult, you wouldn't get the feeling that makes it all worthwhile. What is the point of life if you don't take a few risks?

So what stops people? It comes in many guises but it comes back to one word. Fear. Fear of starting on the bottom rung in a new business, fear of losing your statutory redundancy entitlements, the fear that you might not like the position as much as you think you will. Maybe just fear of the unknown: 'I hate it here but I don't know what to do.' All of these fears are realistic. But working in a job you dislike is soul-destroying.

But I Can't Move

Everyone's situation is different. You may be reading this, thinking, 'I can't move, I've three little mouths to feed!' I understand that. There were sacrifices I made to survive over the past few years that I just couldn't have made if I'd had children. There was no way, for example, that I could have converted my vacant office into a bedsit and moved in there.

But don't rule out change because you can't afford it. Do the maths. There are two ways of making ends meet in any household. One is via the revenue coming in and the other is via expenses. If the revenue drops, you need to cut the expenses. If you were to change direction and accept a lower salary, could you save on travel and childcare? I was able to save €3,000 a month when I moved out of my house – €2,000 on the rent and the rest on travelling and not having to run a house. And by working so close to home, I gained an extra two hours a day that would otherwise have been spent commuting. Living close to where you work can give a huge boost to your quality of life.

Go through all of the money-saving possibilities in Chapter Two. Could you change your mortgage to interest-only for a period of time? Do you have personal loans that will finish soon, or that could be cleared? By thoroughly assessing your costs, there may be enough potential to negate a big decrease in income.

I'll explain how that can work. Let's say the change you have in mind involves a drop in income of €10,000. The first thing you need to do is look at the after-tax difference, because that ten grand drop may not be half as startling as it looks at first. Let's say the after-tax difference is €7,000. (It's going to be different for everyone. I'm just using round figures.) That works out at €583 per month. Where can you cut back to make up as much of that €583 as possible? Do you have car loans you could clear? Suppose you have a car loan with €6,000 owing and two years to run, giving monthly payments of €275. In clearing the loan or selling the car you've brought the net difference back to around the €300 mark.

Where else can you save? Do you have the top satellite TV package? Have you looked at all your costs? Broadband? Landline? Mobile? Gas? Electricity? Groceries? Insurance? Get your bank statement and go through everything. Could you do with one car instead of two? So much of our money goes straight from our employers to service providers via standing orders without our ever seeing it. You'd think we would look at these a lot more often. Go through every-thing you're spending regularly and make sure you're not letting money go in areas you don't need to. And maybe, like our parents' generation, you should start paying attention to the pennies so that the pounds take care of themselves. When you take your eye off the ball, money flies out of your pocket.

For example: I went into Marks & Spencer earlier today for the meal deal for two. What incredible value. A great main course, a side of vegetables, a bottle of wine and a dessert. All for €12.50. Amazing. But the deal wasn't on today, so I just grabbed some lunch for myself. A salmon fillet and a bag of stir-fry veg (I'm in a healthy frame of mind these days . . . pushing on and all that).

'Thank you, sir, that's €X.'

I paid it without thinking, but had expected to get back a tenner plus change from my twenty-euro note. Instead, it was a fiver plus change. I thought she'd made a mistake, so I checked the receipt and it said €10.18. What had happened here? I went in for a two-course meal for two and a bottle of wine for €12.50 and I left with lunch for one and no wine for over a tenner.

Marks & Spencer: 1
Bargain Hunter: 0

In Dax Café Bar we have a chef making our daily special, for which we charge €12.50 to €13.50. So spending more than a tenner on food from a supermarket for something I'm going home to cook seems wrong. If you're on a tight budget you need to be vigilant about things like this. It's as important as what you're earning. Look at Ryanair. They're as profitable as they are because they manage to pare costs to the bone.

My point is that taking a big reduction in salary may not be as impossible as it appears at first glance. Is it worth it to have less money and cut back on a few things, but finish your working day with a smile on your face?

Where to Start

What if you really don't know what you want to do? Suppose the only thing you're sure of is that your existing job just isn't for you. Ask yourself a few questions. What is your passion? Have you got one? If it's not all about the money, what are your hobbies? Is there a potential job that uses those skill sets? Would something that benefits other people in some way give you a greater sense of accomplishment? Are you a great listener? A great communicator? Are you good with your hands? Are you good with technology? Go through all of your skills. Chat to the people who know you best. Sometimes things that you are oblivious to are absolutely obvious to everyone else.

Now it's time to do some research. You may not have a eureka moment immediately. Back in 2002 when I was looking for business ideas, it was research over a number of months that led me to the conclusion that mortgages were the way forward. I started out with a completely different intention. So take your time. Set out particular times for your research. If you don't allocate set times to it, it won't get done.

Another great research option is simply to call people up and talk to them. You'll be amazed by how receptive Irish people are to simply being asked. I do this all of the time. Suppose we're thinking about advertising in a particular medium. We'll take a look and see who's there at the moment, then just pick up the phone and ask them how it's going for them. Not our direct competitors obviously, but the simple truth is that people in general like helping each other out if they're asked. So if you're thinking about a certain area of work and want to find out more, either call in or ring and have a chat with someone who's where you think you'd like to be. It's worth hours of research.

Information and Advice

These days, there's so much information at your fingertips. There are any amount of websites, all run by different bodies: *www.careerdirections.ie* is supported by FAS, *www.qualifax.ie* is run by the Department of Education and *www.bluebrick.ie* by the Institutes of Technology. A handy website to start off with is *www.careersportal.ie.* This brings together a huge range of occupations, training courses and career information and is supported by a wide range of public and private sector organizations. There's also *www.careerguidance.ie*, a privately run website that gives details on guidance teachers and all kinds of training courses and education opportunities.

There's so much information and so much of it is free. You can even get the lecture notes from MIT online if you fancy yourself a new Will Hunting. If you want to self-improve, the obstacles of yesteryear are no longer there.

Retraining may, of course, be an issue. There are thousands of courses out there, from professional qualifications to full degrees. For those on social welfare, the Back to Education Allowance or the Vocational Training Opportunities Scheme will allow you to keep your benefits and return to education, so fees shouldn't be an issue. Check out these websites for more information: *www.studentfinance.ie* and *www.citizensinformation.ie*. Remember, putting in the effort now will have an enormous effect on the quality of your life in the future.

Although it may sound like you've gone back to school, having a chat with a career guidance counsellor is a good idea. Sometimes, a fresh pair of eyes or ears is exactly what's needed. Having a chat with a good recruitment consultant is another great way of getting advice, as well as information on positions that may be available. Some of the sites above have lists of career guidance counsellors, or check *www.igc.ie*, which is the website of the Institute of Guidance Counsellors.

Next Steps

You need to put a lot of work into analysing all of the information before you can make an informed call. Whatever it is you want to do, you have to make sure you have a passion for it. You're going to have to dedicate a lot of your time to getting yourself to a position where you can land the role. After that, you're going to spend a big portion of your life working in that area. When you're looking at career change and are worried about starting on the bottom rung, it's easy to overlook the fact that an awful lot of your skills may be transferable. You need to write them all out and examine each one to see how it might apply to the field you're transferring into.

It's happened to me a few times. I've hired people with

little experience in some areas. Then, when I'm looking to get something done and don't know where to start, they'll say, 'I can do that,' and it will turn out that they have skills I never knew about. Not every skill you have will be transferable, but the skills you have built up that are not directly transferable may have a use at a later stage.

The other point is that starting on the bottom rung is temporary, and there's no harm starting there, especially if someone takes you under their wing and gives you a chance to soak everything up and learn as much as possible. If you have a passion for what you do, you may not be on the bottom rung for long.

The fear of losing your entitlements and/or a good pension scheme and a tax-free lump sum in a few years is a valid fear. The only way to work out the best course of action is to sit down and write out all of the pros and cons. What are your pension entitlements? What are they if you leave now? As much as money motivates me – and it does – I would hate the idea of fear stopping me leaving something I don't want to do.

The fear of not liking the position as much as you thought is an altogether easier one to sort. You need to go and do some voluntary or part-time work in that area to make sure that it's for you. Once you've answered that question, the decision makes itself. Remember that these huge jumps are only scary from this side, never after you've jumped.

8

I Want to be Self-Employed

When I was young and first decided I wanted to run my own business, I spent a long, long time trying to come up with a completely new product. Because I'm not an inventor, and because I'm also useless at technology, that time was wasted. The best completely new invention I have come up with is breakfast dessert. Millions of years of evolution and no one ever came up with breakfast dessert. Go figure.

Anyway, I may have been influenced in thinking I needed to invent something by a story I heard about an Irish businessman who called his yacht 'EKOY 1'. The name was simply '1 Yoke' backwards. He called it '1 Yoke' because that was all he invented. One little yoke. He then patented it and it changed his life. I still don't know what the yoke was for but that was how I understood going into business for yourself. You invent something and it's like winning the Lotto.

But that's not how it worked out for me. Along with the majority of business people, I sell products or variations on products that have been around for a long time. So my eureka moments are not about inventing but about taking something that's already there and improving it and/or spotting gaps that other people have not seen.

These ideas come to me in a few ways. Research is one; looking at a range of potential business areas, other companies and other industries and then speaking to as many people as I can about my idea, challenging it and testing the water to see what works. The more research you do, the clearer everything becomes. A lot of the time it becomes really clear after a while that it is either not a good idea, or it's a good idea for you. Another way ideas come is by being out and about and meeting people, because you never know what a discussion can turn into. You never know what can make you start looking into something you had not previously known about or considered. Travelling is a great way of finding new ideas. When you're abroad you can see things that are taking off in other countries that will hit here in only a matter of time. In Australia, smoothie bars and gourmet healthy burgers seemed to be popular for years before they arrived here. In West Coast America they have had burrito places for years.

The point is that these ideas don't come to you if you are not looking for them. Research and meetings are basically about gathering facts. For a lot of us, me included, when you are weighing up your options and doing your research, the ideas and businesses you keep coming back to are the ones you know best; the ones where you have gained a lot of your experience and contacts.

The eureka moments can happen any time, but for me it's usually just before I fall asleep or just after I wake up in the morning. I used to keep a notepad and pen by the side of the bed. The notebook has now been replaced by the notes section in my iPhone. I used to use the voice recorder, but when you record an idea at 4 a.m., listening back to it the next day, you sound like you have the crazy.

So the notes section in my iPhone is always full. Half of this book is in there, as well as half the marketing ideas for the businesses we have. If I don't write an idea down there and then, it's usually gone.

So you don't need to invent a new Dyson, or Facebook, to set up in business. If you can find a product or service, or a variation of a product or service, or a way of delivering it that saves people money or hassle, that is as good a reason as any to set up in business.

I get a real buzz out of this part of it, the ideas part; how to differentiate yourself from your competitors, how to market yourself right. Sales are the lifeblood of an organization and if you have your marketing and PR right, the sales should flow in. You don't get it right all of the time. Even if you're really good at it, you may get only 70 per cent of it right. Remember, when you don't get it right, change tack and get straight back on the horse. Henry Ford once said, 'I know only half of my advertising works. The problem is, I don't know which half.'

If you can get a product or a service that makes people react to an advert or a call to action, you're onto a winner. But to grow rapidly in spaces that are already well occupied, you need to find a way to launch a better product, or to find a way to deliver your product or service faster or more cheaply. Alternatively, you must be able to save people hassle. Don't ever underestimate what saving people hassle can do. The Holy Grail is when you come up with a product that makes people tell each other about it.

This is the best and most profitable advertising you can do: word of mouth.

Being MD I

Being an employer or a Managing Director, like most careers, becomes a way of life after a while. It's a really intimidating experience deciding to go it alone and, really, it's not for everyone. Trading security for potential gain, deciding to give up a regular pay cheque in search of greater riches, is one of the hardest decisions you'll ever make. But once you're there, you can't ever imagine going back. I've had this experience twice in my life. Once when I was twenty-two, and then again when I came back from Australia in 2001 and started up a new company.

When you're the boss, you're the last to get paid. Everyone gets their salary before you. If there's anything left over after you've paid everyone, that's your slice. When it's bad, it's really bad. I spent two years working the hardest I could possibly work and no matter what I tried, at the end of each month, instead of getting paid, I had to lodge my own money to my business accounts to keep everything afloat. When the crisis hit, there were two months in a row when I had to lodge €35,000 just to pay the salaries. But for years before that, I could take as many holidays as I wanted, I could buy nice cars and clothes. I had the freedom to go wherever and whenever I wanted. So when it is good, it's amazing. And that's only one side of it. There are very few things in the working world quite like having an

idea, a eureka moment, scribbling it down and then deciding to go hell for leather at it and turning it into a successful
business. It is an incredible feeling and something which
makes you jump out of bed each morning to go to work
and get stuck in. That's the part that puts a smile on your
face. (Though the money is bloody great, too.)

The Great Mistake

The biggest mistake people make when they are self-
employed is thinking that they are entitled to a salary. You're
not. In becoming self-employed, you have forgone that
entitlement. You are entitled to anything you bring in over
your costs. If you work it any other way, you will go bust.

I've often seen this scenario: the business is in trouble
and goes looking for investment. They've set up with a
bank loan and, a lot of the time, with money from a par-
ent, and the first thing they set up is their salary. I've queried
this and generally the answer is, 'Well, that's what I need to
live on.' I've never invested in anyone who has done that.
You are not entitled to a salary until you are bringing in
more than your outgoings.

The second big mistake is not controlling costs. In a
nutshell, you need to know exactly what your costs are.
This tells you what your income needs to be. Don't stop
until you hit that mark. The first thing you set up is an Excel
spreadsheet with your business expenses. Rent, mobile
phone, electricity, insurance, printing, etc., etc. That total is
your first basic target. The key to getting to that point as
quickly as possible is reviewing your lifestyle and keeping
your living costs as low as is possible.

If your wife or partner is earning, you could decide that both of you live off the partner's salary or as close to it as possible for a certain period of time. If you can keep your living costs to a minimum, you have a really good chance of making it. This is the make-or-break time. Savings disappear really, really quickly when there's no money coming in.

When I set up in 2002, I had my house rented out and I rented a room in another place for €400 a month. This meant I could keep my living costs to about a grand while I was setting up. Your target is the figure on that Excel spreadsheet. You have to keep a close eye on that and know exactly what you have to bring in each month to break even. Once your sales are greater than the figure at the bottom of that spreadsheet, you have a business. This is a really handy way of keeping an eye on what is paid and not due. When any bills come in, put them in the month that they are due and, when they're paid, move them to the 'Paid' column. A lot of businesses don't know where they are each month because they don't keep an eye on things like these. This is a simple way of controlling your accounts, and you don't need to be an accountant or to have purchased any accounts software to make it work.

Remember that most everyone you speak to for advice will try and sell you something. They will tell you that you can't do without whatever they're selling. The professions are as bad as anyone for this. It's really important to find good, inexpensive professional advisers.

Get a cheap computer or a second-hand one off someone you know, get a cheap phone system. Print your business cards online. None of these things makes sales. You do. The most important part of the package is you.

The cost of setting up a business is now lower than it has been for a lifetime. You can get an office in town for about a third of the price it was a few years ago. I have offices in Dublin 2 that I let out for €600 per month, all in. The tenants have no rates, electricity or heating bills. All in all, one of the most important pieces of advice you can get when setting up is to make every penny a prisoner. Don't let them escape. Most successful business people are great at controlling costs. Always get credit terms. Ask for sixty days, then put it on your credit card. You now have ninety days' credit. If they don't do credit, move to the next company. Haggle the hell out of people. Ask for your first advert for free. I used to wreck advertising sales people's heads.

'No, John, we can't do free adverts.'

My response was, 'If it works, we'll do one every week.'

And if the advert did work, we kept our word and ran it every week. If you can't get an advert for free, which is a good bit of the time, get a really low first-time offer for a run of adverts. You now have your agreed price, so when they try to increase, get them to give you the same deal again for another run. Now you have a really good chance of holding them to it for an extended time.

Negotiating in business doesn't mean you're tight. In fact, the tougher you are about costs, the more kudos you get because when the person you are dealing with is dealing with their supplier, they're doing the same thing. They are under the same pressures as you and they know how tough it is keeping the bottom line in the black. I ask for discounts on everything in and outside of business. If I'm buying a suit, I'll ask for a discount. The best deals that come by are the ones you are cheeky enough to ask for. If you don't ask, you won't get it.

Once you've got over the initial costs, the lifestyle thing still remains the biggest threat to your business. Too many people get a few good months, then head out and get the car and start spending the money that should be going into a reserve fund. This is another major reason businesses fail. You need to save for a rainy day because the rainy day will come, and by then the money has been used to finance the owner's ever-increasing ego and appetite for more and more expensive items. This is the story of so many businesses around town.

Another major cause of business failure is gambling on future earnings. You have to be very calculating when spending money that is not in the bank account. I don't mind spending money that I am 90 per cent sure is coming in – I've used that system to expand rapidly. But I won't gamble the future of the company on it.

Suppose I see an area that's profitable. Let's say a staff member costs €2,500 per month and the advertising costs €2,500. Suppose they are bringing in €10,000-worth of business per month. As soon as I see that, I'll have a new staff member hired and start increasing the advertising budget immediately. I'll start spending the profit to try and turn the €10,000 income into €20,000. Then, I'll hire another member of staff, increase advertising again, and I'll keep on going. This is how we've managed to expand rapidly without the aid of a huge lump sum.

The other key to it is to train your first person really well and then get them training the new staff member, and so on. Number one trains number two, number two trains number three, etc. The two most important things are keeping a really close eye on all of the expenses and getting really good staff. Bad staff make your life a misery. Good staff make your life better and better.

Alone or in Partnership?

One of the important things to consider is whether to go into a partnership or go it alone. There are pros and cons to both. When you set up by yourself, you have total control and there is no chance of falling out with your fellow directors. But two or three heads are better than one, and can allow progress to happen far more quickly. They can have specialities (especially expensive specialities) you don't have. But on the downside, a lot of partnerships do not work out. A partnership break-up, like the ending of any relationship, can be very difficult, and even more difficult to get out of. I was three or four months into developing a partnership with someone recently when it became obvious to me that we would not get on, so I called a halt.

You're probably going to spend even more time with your business partner than with your girlfriend or boyfriend, so make sure you know who you are getting into bed with. But when you get it right, it can be infinitely better than setting up by yourself, especially if you can go into business with someone who is strong in areas where you are weak, and vice versa. That balance can be invaluable.

Legal Structure

So you have decided to set up. That's it, the decision is made. There's no harm in having a chat with an accountant to advise you on whether setting up as a sole trader or as a limited company is the way forward. A limited company offers you more protection if things do not work out, but really you need individual advice to determine the best structure for you. Only recently, legal changes have been brought in to allow you to get a company up and running in a few days, and on your own, too, which is a great development. Google 'cheap company formations' and a load of them will come up.

If you are setting up a new limited company with a partner, a 50/50 split is not my preference. Someone should have the extra 1 per cent that gives the majority and therefore the voting right. You never know what's down the road and, if you need to make a decision in a difficult situation, that 1 per cent gives one of you the power to break a stalemate. This really needs to be established at the outset, as it's difficult to get agreement on anyone taking a lower stake after an agreement to go 50/50 has been settled. But, in my opinion, someone needs to have the controlling share.

Now is a perfect time to set up a shareholder agreement and set out what happens in the event of the partnership splitting up. If you can get a good price from a solicitor to sort this out, great, but agree a fee in advance and have one solicitor advise you all equally. The shareholder agreement is the business equivalent of a pre-nuptial agreement. I've seen a lot of partnerships split up, so this bit is essential.

If you can't get a solicitor to do it cheaply, there are free shareholder-agreement templates online. These may not be as watertight as using a firm of solicitors, but if you don't have the budget, I would still put some sort of agreement in place.

Half of being in business is knowing who to listen to and when, because if you listen to everyone and let them charge you accordingly, you won't have a business. Anytime I have let people charge me on a time basis rather than an agreed fee, it has not worked out well for me. And what I mean by not worked out well for me is I've got a shockingly large bill.

Being MD II

So, you've set up and you are now the Managing Director of your company. It does not matter how long you have been operating, when you meet people, you confidently introduce yourself as the Managing Director of ABCD Enterprises. This is really strange at first, saying that you are a Managing Director; you will nearly feel like you are fraudulently representing yourself. When I set up, I felt as though I had to qualify it. 'I'm sort of a Managing Director,' or 'I'm the Managing Director but I have only just set up.'

Bullshit. You made the hard decision, you set up the company so therefore you arc the MD. And the fact that you are the MD opens doors that were previously closed. People respond better to you being the MD because you've had the balls to set up by yourself. Now it's all about selling yourself and your company. Your job is to represent yourself as professionally as possible and introduce your service or product to as many people as possible. You should be selling and promoting at all times. Remember the power of PR. The better you portray yourself, the more business comes your way.

Let's say you live in Lucan and you work from home. You're asked, 'Where do you work?' You can say the same thing and portray yourself in two very different ways.

A) 'I work from home.'
B) 'My offices are in Lucan.'

If I was working from home, I would never let a prospective sale know this because, regardless of how good you are, you sound like a minnow. If it makes you feel more established, you can get a virtual office for next to nothing in Dublin 2, or the best address convenient to you. A virtual office allows you to have a good business address and any number of additions like a phone-answering service, boardroom for hire, fax number, etc. Shop around for these services, because there is a lot of competition and a big difference in price. It's also worth looking at places like The Digital Hub, where there is a pool of services and offices available.

Get a Management Accountant

The essential bit of advice I would give anyone setting up is to get a good and reasonably priced management accountant. If you're stuck, email me and I'll give you a name. There is a big difference between a management accountant and a normal accountant. What you want in the first place is someone who can teach and mentor you on the running of the business and, secondarily, to do the accounts. The really important bit is the running of the business. If you get a good management accountant, they will have been at the embryo stage with hundreds of small businesses. They will be able to teach you the fundamentals of running a company and implementing all of the systems you need to have in place. It's amazing what you don't know until you sit down with someone who points it all out to you. And you really need someone who has done it all before to set you targets and to tell you when you're not hitting them, and that you're not working hard enough. If it's your first time being self-employed, you will not be the best person to assess that. You could be working fourteen hours a day, concentrating on the wrong areas, getting no sales and heading for disaster. You could be heading home each evening thinking you are doing everything you can when, in fact, you're actually doing the opposite. The best decision I made when I set up my first company was to hire a management accountant. He set me goals and made me deliver a sales report each week. For a while, I was a bit put out by this, especially when I didn't hit my target and was questioned on why.

'Who do you think you are?' I used to think. 'I'm the boss.'

But everyone, even the boss, needs targets that they have to stick to. Employing someone to make sure you do your job is money well spent. As far as I'm concerned, self-regulation means no regulation, in this, or any other area of life.

Finance

Once you have worked out what capital you need to set up, you will most likely need to get a loan. With the banking system in the state it is in at the moment, business loans are very difficult to obtain. But not impossible.

I set up First Credit with €40,000 and a €20,000 overdraft. Looking back, I think I could have done it with fewer funds, because it was only when I was out of cash that the real pressure started and I concentrated on getting in the minimum amount I needed to cover costs each month. I remember looking at a bank account which was €19,800 overdrawn and thinking, 'The fun starts here. You need €3,200 in by the end of the month or you don't have a business.'

Four years later, I had eighteen staff and we were making a gross profit of over €100,000 a month. Four years after that, mortgage brokering as a business was effectively gone and I was back to where I started with no staff and looking for €3,000 a month to cover costs! I had new ventures to keep me sane, but it is heartbreaking to spend six years building something from an idea, only to watch helplessly as it disintegrates around you. But, as I've said before, them's the breaks. I'm not the only one this has happened to. The career path I chose has huge highs and desperate lows. When my last employee handed in his notice, it was a strange moment. He was working in a miserable job so as not to let me down, and I was continuing to work in a miserable job to keep him employed. It was really emotional because his leaving meant it was over.

But then it felt like my shoulders got lighter. Five minutes after he resigned I thought to myself, 'Fucking hell I can go on a holiday! I've no salary to pay at the end of the month. I can sell the company, I can leave it dormant for a year or two, I can do whatever I want now!'

There was a real feeling of freedom that came with that. In retrospect, I should have made him redundant and given him a cash lump sum, but the motivating factor at the time was that there did not seem to be any other jobs to go to.

That was six months ago. I rebranded the company, removed myself from the day-to-day running, hired staff that know nothing about mortgages and changed the focus of the business to life assurance. First Credit is now a small growing company again, except we don't arrange mortgages.

But getting finance right now is tough. I applied to my bank for a €250,000 loan two years ago in order to buy one of my competitors. I got a phone call to say I was approved.

'That's great,' I said.

'There is one condition,' the friendly bank person said. 'We need a cash security of €250,000.'

'I'm not familiar with cash security,' I said.

'Well, it's cash on deposit,' I was told.

'So I have to lodge €250,000 with you for you to lend it back to me?'

'Yes, that's basically it.'

It's a sign of the times, I suppose. In previous years the same bank had lent me, within reason, whatever I asked for.

Going for that loan is the biggest pitch of your business life. If you don't get past Go, you can't collect the €200. You need a comprehensive business plan, showing a detailed profit and loss. The main benefit is that this shows you have given it a lot of thought and you know what you are getting into. Bring any proof or details of where the revenue is going to come from. Bring in your CV, detailing your experience in the field. Make sure you show that you are putting in your own money.

These days, I can work out a business plan on the back of a packet of cigarettes. (I'll have to borrow the pack now, though, because I don't smoke any more.) I'll know whether it's worth going after or not, but that's because I've done it plenty of times before. A business plan for a novice will show you a lot of the incidentals you won't think of your first time around. There are plenty of free business-plan templates online.

If the bank turns you down, which is likely, you need to log onto *www.creditreview.ie*. The Credit Review Office is a state-run body that will allow you to appeal the decision if you are a small or medium-sized enterprise (SME) that has been declined credit. The office has no power to force the banks to lend but they say that, to date, the banks have complied with their opinions, and this applies to start-ups as well as existing companies. So it's definitely worth getting them to review your case if you have been declined. In fact, I would say that you should assume this is the whole process. If it is anything like the way banks deal with their obligations in terms of the ombudsman, it might be the only way to get money from them. As I have seen many times, the only way the banks in this climate will really do anything they don't want to is when they are told to. I have seen cases of glaring decisions against the customer which any reasonable person would agree to, but the bank would deny, deny and deny, hoping the customer would just give up. In most cases they do. So you should consider it as par for the course. Apply to the bank, get turned down and then go to the Credit Review Office for the real decision. The Credit Review Office only deals with AIB and Bank of Ireland, which are the only NAMA banks left for business loans. If you want *www.creditreview.ie* to review your case, you need to provide them with your details in writing, together with the full application and the decline letter if applicable.

State Supports

Enterprise Ireland is there to help companies who plan to export goods and services: companies who wish to grow globally. Your local enterprise board may be able to help with feasibility studies and, possibly, with grants. There are a good few other regional initiatives which are worth checking out, like Shannon Development for the Shannon region, Udaras na Gaeltachta for Gaeltacht areas, and Intertrade Ireland for cross-border. I don't want it to sound like they're throwing money around, because they aren't. Anytime I went looking for some, it was not available.

However, depending on your product and where you want to trade, you may be exactly what they want to back.

Although grants may be hard to come by, support can come in many ways, not least in mentoring and advice. For this, talk to your local university or college. Venture capitalists – like on *Dragons' Den* – offer an investment in return for a percentage in your company.

If you are unemployed, you may be eligible for the Back to Work Enterprise Allowance, or the Short-Term Enterprise Allowance. Under these schemes, it's possible to get extra help with training, market research, business plans and even loans to buy small items of equipment. There's also a non-profit company called *www.first-step.ie* who provide micro-finance (loans of up to €25,000), and also a handy little website, *www.nubie.com*, which gives information on everything that someone setting up needs to know.

Christening Your Business

Picking your name is one of those time-consuming jobs that, when you get it right, is another eureka moment. My basic priority was to sound established. So I picked the name 'First Credit' for my mortgage company and 'Pembroke Insurances' for my corporate insurance brokerage. Both sound like they have been around for a hundred years. Another good option is to include what you do in your company name. This can be pretty handy for a number of reasons, not least when people are searching for you on the net. Sometimes, you can have a name that is none of the above, but fits exactly what you're doing. When we came up with *www.quotedevil.ie* 'for a hell of a quote', with a little devil saying it, we knew we were onto a winner.

Answering the Phone

Even if you're only a one-man operation, you need to answer the phone like you're established and a large company. Never let the phone ring more than four times. When I ring a number and get an answering machine during working hours, I automatically assume they are a Mickey Mouse operation. In the days before telephone answering companies, I used to redirect the landline to my mobile and, when I answered, I'd try not to sound as though I was out and about and, therefore, a one-man band. Many times I would be out on the street and I could see the office was diverting to my mobile, so I would duck into the nearest shop and answer, 'Hello, First Credit, John speaking.'

I must have looked like a right flute running into the Spar and answering as though I was sitting at a desk in an office but, either way, perception is reality, and the people on the other end of the phone did not know I was answering mortgage questions by the ice cream machine in the Spar. Other times, at my desk this time, I'd answer the phone (within four rings) and I might get, 'Oh John, did I get straight through to you?'

All of my ads gave the impression of a large company

with loads of advisers. Little did the customer know the sum total of First Credit in 2002 was me, a plant (now deceased), an old, slow PC and a kettle.

That First Call

One of my most vivid memories of that time was waiting for that first call. I'd put all of this money, time and energy into setting up, into the brand, the name, the phone system, the professional indemnity insurance (which was €11,000), the systems, getting an office in town with a good address, doing so much to sound established, becoming regulated, etc., then creating an advert and putting it into a national newspaper. Then I was waiting by the phone for a call. And waiting, and waiting. The longer it went on, the more I thought, 'What have I done? I've sold a house and spent thousands on this ad campaign and there are no calls.'

This went on all day, and the next day, then the day after that the advert went out again and it was the same thing. No calls . . . So, I'm getting ready to go home on the third day when, *Rrrring!* I can't contain my excitement. The phone has barely rung and I'm all over it. 'Hello, John here from First Credit, how can I help?' I can't get the words out fast enough.

'Hello, I just saw your advert in the newspaper.'

I jump up and furiously start punching the air like I've won a world title fight. It's worked, it's worked, it's worked!

'Well, this is Brian here from *The Star*. I was wondering if I could tell you about our advertising rates . . .'

Boom . . . my stomach, heart and everything else hit the floor. All of that work and effort and the only call I get is from someone trying to sell me something. I went home that night after another fourteen-hour day, completely despondent and disillusioned. I came back the next day and the next day and eventually found other avenues that started to work. In the early days, my best advertising was ringing people as opposed to waiting for the phone to ring. Later on, print advertising worked well. I'm telling you this because if you ever set up by yourself, you will become familiar with the absolute elation of taking a gamble and seeing it work. You will also become familiar with feeling as though everything is falling apart and your stomach hitting the floor when it looks like it's not working. A lot of the time, the two feelings may only be days, maybe even minutes apart. Only the strong willed survive and, when I say that, I mean the people who can come back for a fight the day after getting the absolute stuffing knocked out of them. They're the ones who will succeed.

9

I Want to Live to be 100

This is not the chapter of the book I most looked forward to writing, but it may actually be the most important. We associate pensions with the blue-rinse brigade at the Post Office. They are not in any way glamorous or sexy. This also means that people don't pay as much attention to them as they should. But they are an absolute necessity. Maybe we should turn this on its head and PR them. We could change their name to the 'Double-Your-Money Fund' and get Jennifer and Brad to promote them . . . Maybe I'm a bit out of date there . . .

When you put money into a pension, it goes in before tax. So, in practice, if you are on the higher rate of tax, you can double your money even if it makes no return ever, because you have just saved yourself the income tax and PRSI. I suppose it's technically wrong to say it doubles your money – it actually saves your money from being halved. It works like this: say you earn €100 and you're on the higher rate of tax. That means that between tax and PRSI, you only get €50 approximately in your hand. But if you put that €100 into a pension, it stays at €100. The pension saves your cash from being halved. If you're on the lower rate of tax, the pension saves your cash from being reduced by a third.

The way life expectancy is going, you need to figure out what you're going to do for money for the twenty, thirty or even forty years after you retire. I saw a survey recently that said 50 per cent of adults under forty-five had no pro-visions made for retirement. Fifty per cent! The reality is that if you want to have any quality of life after you retire, you cannot depend on the state pension. In Ireland right now, the non-contributory state pension is €219 per week, payable from age sixty-eight, up from age sixty-five. By the time the current generation of workers gets to retirement, the qualifying age could be higher again. And with our age-ing population, the country may not be able to pay the state pension in years to come. This does not even take into account the fact that the National Pension Reserve Fund is being used to shore up the shortfall in government funds.

You hear people knocking pensions regularly – sometimes with good reason – but the tax breaks mean there is no better investment. The pension fund also grows tax free. If you have money on deposit, you have to pay Deposit Interest Retention Tax (Dirt Tax) on the interest each year. Individual shares or stocks are subject to capital gains tax, managed funds have exit tax. Pensions are the most tax-efficient investment you can make.

The younger you start, the less you have to pay in as you get closer to retirement age, so starting early saves you a fortune down the road.

When I was in my early twenties and a financial adviser,

my most lucrative work by far was on a very large pension scheme for a company with over a hundred staff. It took me about two weeks to do the full review for every individual staff member, but those two weeks made up a large portion of my earnings for the year. Even though it was far and away my most lucrative work, I absolutely hated those two weeks. I used to dread them because it was fourteen days of tedium, working out performance, contributions, benefits . . . I've since learned to always outsource this kind of thing because it's not my forte, but those days I would not let anyone else do it. So, yes, pensions are boring, but that's the way they should be. They should be safe, conservative and boring. If your pension was a person, it should be a middle-aged, grey-faced man who won't make you a millionaire but won't lose you everything. It should not be a twenty-three-year-old hotshot in a flashy suit who might make a million but could just as quickly lose everything.

Self-Administered Pensions

Over the past few years, pension contracts have become increasingly sophisticated, especially with the arrival of self-administered schemes. These allow the individual paying into the pension to effectively assume the role of fund manager and make the investment decisions himself; whether to buy individual shares, or a property he has his eye on, etc.

One of the key principles of sound investment is spreading

the risk: the idea that whatever the size of your investment, it will be spread over a wide range of different areas. When you decide to go the self-administered pension route, you have opted out of this shared-risk approach and decided that you are likely to make more money than the fund investment manager. I'm sure there are success stories out there but an awful lot of people got wiped out by assuming control of their pensions. They used their fund to buy property and bank shares. For the most part, unless you are a sophisticated full-time or active investor, this approach is not for you. You really need to be a certain type of person and have plenty of time on your hands to make a success of it. For most people, your standard company pension plan or Personal Retirement Savings Account (PRSA) is the way forward. I'll explain why, hopefully without making you fall asleep.

How Pensions Work

Very simply, you pay an amount each month, let's say €100. That monthly contribution buys investments on your behalf, from low to high risk depending on your choice and, at the end of your working life, there is enough money there to give you a tax-free (at least it's tax free at the moment) lump sum and an income for the rest of your life. The insurance company has hundreds of thousands of other people also putting in money each month. The pension fund invests this money in a wide range of areas that may not be available to the small investor. One of the main benefits of this approach is it spreads the risk in a cost-effective manner.

Here's an example. Let's say you want to invest €100 each month. The fees involved in buying such a small amount mean that you would need a huge return from that €100 to make it worthwhile. Instead, you invest your €100 in a pension fund, and the fund spreads that €100 across a wide range of investments.

This approach also reduces the risk. Let's say you buy €100 of stock in American Airlines and then their pilots go on strike. You're goosed. But if you invested in a diversified fund, if the same pilots go on strike, yes, that individual stock gets hammered, but it has a negligible effect on your fund.

Over the past few years, many people close to retirement and even after retirement have had the value of their pension funds annihilated. This is where the value of the fund drops, so your pension could go from being worth €300,000 to €200,000 almost overnight. If you are close to retirement, you should not be in a high-risk fund. If you want to be in a high-risk fund for potentially higher returns, you should do this only when you're young.

And if you are young, don't panic when pension funds get annihilated, because this represents a buying opportunity. Let me explain how it works. If the value of the fund has gone down, so has the price of the units you buy each month. It's like buying stocks when the market has dropped. Let's say your pension fund is worth €100,000 and you are putting in €100 every month. This €100 buys you 100 units (like stocks) for €1 each. The market drops and our fund is now worth only €50,000, but your €100 is now buying 200 units each month for 50 cents each. Do you see where I'm going? If the market just goes back to where it was before the drop, you will have made gains because every month you have been buying way more lower-priced units. So a big stock market drop can favour the younger pension investor over the long term.

A collapse in the value of your fund is, however, an absolute nightmare if it happens when you are close to retirement.

Which Scheme to Use?

The best scheme to be in is a company pension scheme. This is because there are two people putting money into your fund, you and your employer, and both of you get tax breaks. There isn't a better fund than one someone else is paying into. The Rolls Royce of company schemes is the defined benefit scheme. This basically means that a salary is guaranteed at retirement for each year you have worked. The investment performance of your fund does not matter to you as it's all to do with years you have worked and your salary. You only really find defined benefit schemes in the public service now. They're quite costly for employers, because if they don't get the investment right, they still have to pay the pension.

The most common type of company pension plan is defined contribution. This is where you and your employer pay a portion into your pension fund and the value of your fund at retirement is dependent on how much you both put in, the investment performance and the length of time you were paying in.

If you don't have a company pension scheme, the pension options are either a personal pension scheme or a PRSA. You've probably heard of PRSAs at this stage. They were brought in to provide a more flexible pension alternative because you can't change between a company and a personal pension; you'd have to stop one and start the other. So, a personal pension is for those who are either self-employed or employed in a company where there is no pension scheme. If, however, you were to become employed by a limited company in a few years, you cannot transfer your personal pension to a company scheme, whereas you can transfer a PRSA.

If you've been self-employed and have a PRSA, you can easily bring the PRSA with you if you become employed, and the employer can begin to contribute to it. So they have great flexibility, and are the best option if you move between companies and periods of self-employment. They are, however, slightly less tax efficient than a company scheme because the Universal Social Charge applies to PRSAs but not to company schemes.

If you have a company pension scheme and you switch jobs, you can move your company fund from one employer scheme to another. If you are in a defined benefit scheme, the Rolls Royce one, and you leave the job, you are better leaving the pension there until retirement. You could get cash value, but you would be mad to move it. There are also buy-out bonds. These allow you to transfer all of the money that was paid into the pension into a bond in your own name, over which you have full control.

AVCs

Another term you've no doubt heard of is the AVC. These are pretty simple, in theory, anyway! An AVC (Additional Voluntary Contribution) effectively allows you to pay more into your pension, over and above what you and your employer are paying in on a regular basis. This way, you can either retire earlier or make up for years you did not contribute to a pension, or fund a higher tax-free lump sum. You get tax relief on the amount you put in, which is limited to between 15 per cent and 30 per cent of your salary, depending on your age. Thirty per cent is a lot of your salary to put into anything and is really for older people making up for lost time.

Fund Performance

The most important issues when deciding which pension company to go with are fund performance and charges. Benjamin Disraeli said, 'There are three kinds of lies: lies, damned lies and statistics.' Nowhere is it truer than when talking about investment performance. You can make anyone look great using statistics. Simply changing the dates of a survey from 1 June to 3 June can completely change a performance comparison. So, do your research carefully, and remember, because something did well last year or the year before, this does not mean it will do well next year.

I'm always wary of the performance of specialist funds

as they are just that, specialist funds. High-risk or specialist funds can make or lose a fortune quite easily. These are funds that invest in a particular area, which could be anything from gold to a particular type of stock, to a particular region. You hear a lot about them when they do well and not so much when they don't. And there is no guarantee that if they did well in the past, they will do well in the future – again, as with any investment, keeping all of your eggs in one basket is a bad idea. Generally, with a specialist fund, the money is all in the one area.

I always look at the company's pedigree and the performance of their signature funds (some companies can have thousands of funds). The other consideration is your appetite for risk and your age. You can get very involved in picking funds, or you can pay an adviser to do it for you. There are also structured funds managed by insurance companies that gradually move you out of high-risk funds as you get older. I choose the funds that comprise my pension. They're spread out across different areas, with varying degrees of risk, but because I'm young (relatively), I have a good chunk in high-risk funds.

Charges

Besides controlling risk, one of the key things to manage at the start of the process is the cost. Like everything else, shop around. There are a few different charges on a pension fund, and if you don't keep your eye on them, you won't get the best deal. The three key charges are the management, commission and allocation charges. The management charge is the charge the pension company levies for managing your money. It can range from 0.6 per cent right up to 3 per cent. A high management charge can eat away at your pension.

The commission can be as high as 50 per cent of the first year's premium, though most good brokers will arrange it for much less than that. You need to make sure that the renewal commission is not too high, either, because if it is, your investment needs to work a lot harder to get growth.

The allocation is the amount of your money that actually goes into the pension. For example, if it's a 95 per cent allocation, then €95 of your €100 goes in each month before charges. The allocation can be as low as 50 per cent in the first year, or as high as 100 per cent. You need to make sure that you get a good deal on all three.

To summarize, the things to look out for are:

A) Allocation year 1
B) Allocation rate for year 2 and subsequent years
C) The initial commission
D) The renewal commission
E) The management charge

If you are doing a pension transfer, make sure the allocation is over 100 per cent, if you can. That may sound strange, but the pension company will give you credit for extra money because they will be taking their charges out of it. You may be able to get higher than 100 per cent. But that's no good if your management charge is 2 per cent, because 2 per cent of €100,000 is over two grand a year.

Big money. As with everything else, there are bad deals, good deals and great deals out there.

The Pension Levy

Speaking of management charges, no chapter on pensions could be complete without going into the 0.6 per cent Pension Levy. Do I agree with it? No. Can you turn it on its head? Yes. The government have put a four-year 0.6 per cent charge onto our pension funds. However, most management fees on older pension funds are far higher than they are on modern pension contracts. Management fees can range from 0.6 per cent to 2 or even 3 per cent in some cases. This is lucrative business for the pension companies and you won't even notice.

So, let's say you're currently paying a management charge of 1.5 per cent of your pension fund, and now the 0.6 per cent charge has been added, giving you a total charge on your fund of 2.1 per cent. By shopping around and seeing what companies will offer, you could reduce your management charge from 1.5 per cent to 1 per cent or even 0.6 per cent, thereby almost negating the impact of the pension fund levy. If you are on a higher management charge, you could be even better off.

If you do this you need to ask the same questions detailed above, just as if you're buying a pension for the first time. And if you're moving your pension from one company to another, you need to make sure all of your money is being transferred and that it is not being eaten up with charges. Effectively, you need to get great allocation so, separate to the investment advice, get quotes on the allocation. This can range from 98 per cent allocation to 104 per cent allocation, so shop around. To reiterate, although 104 per cent may sound strange, the pension company will give you credit for extra money because they'll be taking their charges out of it. Don't be blinded by the high allocation and ignore the management charge or the commission on your monthly premium. Remember, too, that there is likely to be an extra charge to move the pension away from the company within the first five years so, over that period, they'll make back that 4 per cent and more.

If you can get a management charge that is 0.6 per cent lower than you currently pay, then you have just got the pension company to eat up the Pension Levy in full. This really is one of those areas where, if you look after the pennies, the pounds will take care of themselves.

Retiring

When you hit retirement age, there are a number of options, depending on the type of pension you have. At present, depending on your pension type, you can take either a percentage of your salary or 25 per cent of your fund as a tax-free lump sum, and then the remainder buys what's called an annuity, which provides a guaranteed income – basically an interest rate – on the fund you've built up. It's generally a higher interest rate because when you die, the insurance company keeps the fund. The other options are an Approved Minimum Retirement Fund (AMRF) and an Approved Retirement Fund (ARF). Both are basically managed funds from which you take an income while they, hopefully, continue to grow. What you do with the lump sum you have built up over twenty or thirty years requires very careful consideration. There are various restrictions on these funds and a variety of tax implications. All of your options need to be set out on paper and analysed very closely.

There, now, that wasn't so bad . . . was it?

10

I Want to Buy a House

I nearly envy you! You know when you lend someone a book that you loved, and you're slightly jealous because they now have it to look forward to for the first time? Recently, I lent someone the boxed set of *The Wire*. I was delighted to lend it, but still sort of envious of someone else being able to sit down and watch the whole thing through as a completely new experience.

I'm a bit like that about buying your first house. The first one made me so nervous. I felt I was way out of my depth. I didn't know whether it was the right time, I didn't know if I could afford it, I was afraid the market would crash. Would I like living in the area? Would I be able to save the deposit in time? All of these worries have been experienced by everyone who has ever bought a property. But it's such a great feeling when you eventually get the keys and walk into a place and get your head around the fact that this is yours. You own it and no one else. You can play the music loud, you don't need to put clothes on if you're going down to the kitchen for water in the middle of the night. Nobody can put on *Coronation Street* in your house. God, you can even paint a big-ass mural of your face on the wall if you want! And no one can tell you not to, cos it's yours!

I still love buying property, but it's the law of diminishing returns. Because of the range of emotions you go through when you buy your first house, you'll always remember it. Just like your first car. My first car was a 1977 Triumph Spitfire convertible I could barely afford to put petrol in. I was nineteen and I loved it. I took it apart in my parents' back garden and rebuilt it. Ten years afterwards, my father said he could still hear the clunk of the lawnmower blades passing over a piece of the car I had mislaid in the grass. I spent a few years doing it up and respraying it red, I put an engine from a Triumph Dolomite into it and all of my birthday presents for years went towards doing the car up. Without concentrating, I even remember the registration: 618 XZA. Ten years later, I had a stunning convertible Mercedes SL. But can I remember the registration? Not a chance. Your first house is like that. There's nothing like collecting the keys and walking through the door for the first time.

Bricks First, Then Wheels

The first step to owning your own house is setting up a regular savings account. Transferring ad-hoc amounts on a monthly basis does not work half so well, especially with finance as limited as it is at the moment. You need to save a regular amount each month so that you can demonstrate that you are able to repay an amount equivalent to the monthly mortgage repayment over a long period of time. The days of 100 per cent mortgages, or even getting a mortgage purely with a deposit from your parents, are gone. You need to be able to show you can afford the repayment each and every month. If you save for six months and then take it out for a holiday, that won't count. If you're living at home or renting a room, you need to set up a standing order. Giving your landlord or your mum €400 in cash each month won't count. The bank's underwriter, the person who will be deciding whether you get the mortgage or not, has to see everything on paper. In the current climate, all they want is a reason to say no. If the banks could shut up shop and not lend at all, they would. So if you give them a reason to say no, they'll take it.

Forty per cent of your take-home pay needs to be going on rent and savings. If you have a car loan, that can come out of the 40 per cent, too, but make sure you have the loan cleared by the time you're going for a mortgage. Loan repayments have a negative effect on the amount you can borrow. The higher the repayment on a car or personal loan, the less you can borrow. In fact, the biggest obstacle to obtaining a mortgage for first-time buyers is the car or personal loan. So, if you're starting off in your career, LEAVE THE CAR FOR A YEAR OR TWO! Go for the house first, if you can. I didn't, and I know how difficult it is, but when you buy the car, it sucks up so much of your income that it's really difficult to save. There's insurance, tax, petrol ... You'll no doubt knock it off a few things as everyone does when they're starting out, so there are regular bouts of body work, then servicing ...

I realize that owning a car is the first sign to your peers

that you're getting ahead, but it's the one that pulls you back the most when you're in the real business of getting ahead. And once you have a car, you won't ever get rid of it. Stay on your parents' policy for another year or two. And this is coming from a car fanatic, so if you manage it, you're doing a lot better than me. I could not resist buying wheels over bricks, but if you can, it will put you a few years ahead of the posse.

How Much to Borrow

Your next step is to talk to a few banks and mortgage brokers to see what you can afford to borrow. They will be able to advise you on the amount, the rate, the monthly cost, the term and the deposit you will need, which is usually between 8 and 10 per cent of the value of the property. They will also be able to tell you if you're going to be eligible to borrow right now, and if not, they should be able to give you a plan to put in place to borrow in six to twelve months. It may be that you haven't saved enough or for long enough, or it may simply be that you've not been in your present job for long enough. Either way, you can get advice on putting a short-term plan together.

Once you have all of this done, you need to get approval. Not 'approval in principle', where the loan application was looked at and someone said, 'Yeah, that looks fine.' You need to send in all of your paperwork and get approved by the lender you have chosen. As the banks would prefer not to lend, they will take any opportunity to say no, so get your approval before you start house hunting. The bank may tell you that you need a property for them to fully assess your loan. If that's the case, pick an address off *www. daft.ie*, with a price close to the maximum they've told you you'll get, and use that. Once you have the approval, it's game on!

You're nearly always better buying on the best street you can afford. It's much better to buy a smaller house or a house that needs work on the best street you can afford, rather than a bigger, better-decorated property in a poorer location. You can change the decor of a place and make it stunning, but the address always remains the same. If you are a first-time buyer, I would generally buy at the top end of what the bank offers.

There are always exceptions to the rule, however. Right now, the most important part is making sure you can afford the monthly mortgage, taking into account a good few interest rate rises. Why we can't have mortgages structured like other countries, or like certain business leases, is beyond me, where interest rate rises affect the term of the mortgage as opposed to the monthly payment. With this system, if you agree to pay €1,400 a month for twenty-five years at a given rate, interest rate rises push the term out to say 25.6 or 26 years. And if there are rate reductions, the term reduces. This would be hugely beneficial in keeping people out of arrears. But that's another day's work!

In my experience, most people want to live close to where they were brought up. Your average person moves three times in their life; the first property is usually of a size and location that's affordable. Hopefully, over the long term there will be capital appreciation, but if you're also paying back the capital you borrowed on a monthly basis, the amount borrowed is also going down each month. This is what gives you equity. When the value of the property drops below what you borrowed, that's negative equity.

If at all possible in the current climate, it makes sense to take the first two steps in your first go. By that I mean jump past the starter home and onto the second home while you can. Right now, the market is in the condition it was in when I started out; I managed to avoid the two-bed townhouses and went straight for the four-bed semi. Admittedly, as a twenty-three year old, I did look a bit out of place in the middle of a row of families. But it appreciated faster and, even if it didn't, I wouldn't have had to move if I wanted to bring up a family.

I would also advise trying to pay the mortgage over the shortest term you can afford, keeping the payment to around 40 per cent to 45 per cent of your take-home pay. But don't actually commit to the shortest payment period possible with your bank, because this ties your hands. If you get into difficulty, you'll have no option but to refinance. If you take the mortgage out over thirty years but can afford twenty, increase the payments to have it gone in twenty years. That way, you can reduce the overpayment when the rainy days eventually arrive.

Checking Out the Location

Call in to the neighbours for a chat! This may sound strange, but pop in, say hello and tell them that you're thinking of buying next door. See what they're like. If there's a full-on rave happening at 11 p.m. on a Sunday, you'll know it's not for you. This is the best way of getting a feel for a place. People are generally receptive because they've been in this situation themselves. Being beside a green area is generally a really good thing, but if there are lanes and dark alleys around, it's advisable to come back at night-time and check for hoodies.

And if it's an apartment, talk to loads of people in the area and find out what the sound proofing is like. That goes for three-bed semis, too. Poor sound insulation in semi-detached houses has been a problem since I bought my first place . . . Now is as good a time as any to apologize to my neighbours in Bray for the occasional blast of late-night music. I know one of the younger members of my neighbour's family got mortgage advice from First Credit a few years ago and during the process told my staff member that I woke them up occasionally with music after the nightclubs had finished. In my defence, they were very thin walls and I was in my early twenties!

Finding the Sun

You have probably heard the word 'aspect'. What is it and why is it so important? Aspect is simply the direction a house is facing, and it's all about the back garden. South facing is generally considered the best, although my preference is south-west. We are all familiar with Stephen's Green in the summer. You have the Grafton Street side and then the opposite side, the much quieter side. During the summer months, the Grafton Street side is generally bright and sunny whereas, on the opposite side, it's generally dark and shady. If you have a south-facing garden, it will catch the sun like the Grafton Street side whereas, if you have a north-facing garden, it will be dark like the other side of the green. So, if you have a north-facing back garden and want to sunbathe in your bikini on a Friday evening after work, you're going to have to do it in your front garden. That's the reason south-facing gardens are way more sought after. An east-facing garden will get the morning sun and a west-facing garden will get the full evening sun. A south-facing garden will get sun through the middle of the day and the early evening, while a south-west-facing garden will get the best of the afternoon and early evening sun.

An architect friend of mine has a different view. His preference is an east–west orientation, giving him sunlight into his house early in the morning through the front, and in the evening, it comes in via the back garden . . . so south-to-west-facing back gardens are, in my opinion, the best.

The Survey

When you have your sale agreed, you will need to get an architect or a structural engineer to survey the place. Ignore the fact it has Homebond. You need a professional to give it a thorough look through, especially if it's an apartment. Find out about sound insulation and whether it's one of the ones thrown together during the boom, as a lot of these were put together really badly. A good, thorough survey will throw up any negatives, whatever they may be, from build quality to potential problems.

Negotiating

Whether it's boom or bust, the quality of the deal you do is up to you. While economic conditions are a factor, they're not the main factor. You can still do a bad deal in a buyer's market, and a good deal in boom times (they're just much harder to come by). At the height of the boom and within months of each other, I did both the best property deal I've ever done and the worst. So it's not all about timing. It's what you can negotiate.

Because buying a home is an emotive business, trying to stay unemotional while negotiating is nearly impossible. Because of the stress, the time, the work and the research, when you have made the decision to go for the property, there's a tipping point where all of that emotional build-up suddenly hinges on a yes or a no. When it comes back as a no, you'll generally increase your offer instead of holding on, taking your time and seeing what else comes up. Why would you want to wait? You've already been saving for a year and looking for six months!

It's important to recognize what's going on here. You've already pictured yourself in the kitchen on a miserable Monday and out in the garden on a Saturday in June . . . You may have looked at schools and parks for kids to play in, and so on. So, all that emotion has to go somewhere.

And this is when you are at your most weak and, therefore, most susceptible to paying more than you wanted.

It happens so often that the underbidder on a property, the one who loses out, manages to find another property shortly afterwards. Without fail, every single one says, when they have bought somewhere else, that they were really lucky because the new property is far better, and thank God they didn't get the last property. Now, is it the case that almost every underbidder is amazingly lucky afterwards, or is it simply that the emotion, if you will excuse the pun, finds a new home to go to?

So, what can you do to get around that? I generally get someone else to do my bidding for me if I can. This keeps me from getting too excited! But here's what I did for my girlfriend Karen when she was looking to buy. Every time she saw a place she liked, she would – like every other buyer – get really excited, then so disappointed when it didn't work out. The entire process wrecked her head. I decided to leave her completely out of the equation and viewed places for her myself, then only showed her the property once I had a provisional agreement on the price in place. And by provisional, I mean I spoke to the agent before even going to the property and asked about the price. I pointed out that my budget was lower than the asking price and asked them to check whether or not an offer at this level might be acceptable to the owner.

The agent may come back and say, 'I need a firm offer.' You can use the person who isn't there as a negotiating tool. Say, 'This is the budget. Before I bring my partner I need to know if an offer of €X would be acceptable. We are cash buyers and can close in four weeks if you want.'

If a property was advertised at, say, €300K or €400K, I'd speak to the agent first and tell him the budget is whatever amount below the asking price, then ask if there is any point in viewing the property. The answer is either yes or no. If it's absolutely no, then move on to the next one. In the current climate, estate agents are only too willing to agree deals because buyers are thin enough on the ground.

Here are the golden rules on negotiating:

- Have your loan approval sourced.
- Never show your loan approval to an estate agent. Never let them know how much you are approved for.
- Ring and speak to the agent and find out what kind of price they'll take. Tell them your budget and ask if it's worthwhile viewing the house, given that constraint.
- If you are a couple, consider leaving the property search up to the less-emotional one. Or split the viewings evenly between you.
- Don't get too excited when you like a place. Don't allow yourself to get emotional until after you have an agreement in place.
- Don't make a formal offer. Say, 'Can you find out whether they are amenable to doing a deal at X price. If so, we can move to the next step.'
- Don't be afraid to walk away from a property and continue the search. You may just get a call in a few weeks' time, or you may have found somewhere better and cheaper in the meantime.
- You don't have to put a property down when you walk in. Neither is it a good idea to get lyrical about it. Keep the emotions in check until your deal is done.

- Don't restrict your research to the house. Check out the area, the neighbours, everything.
- Find out what you're buying, check the build quality, sound proofing, and so on. The €300 or €400 that this costs will be the best money you can spend.
- If you put down a low offer, the chances are the owner will sit on it for a while. If this is the case, don't be afraid to give them a deadline. Email or write and tell them the offer is only valid until a certain date. Then they have a date by which they must either accept or decline your offer.

Build Your Own

There is a saying that moving house is one of the most stressful things you can do in your life. Well, only a person who has never built a house can say that, because compared to building a house, moving house is a doddle.

A few years ago, buying land and building a house was a way of getting a property for less than market value, and that made up for the hassle involved. Over the past few years, when everyone was earning too much, many tradesmen, builders and architects turned into prima donnas and did not expect to work on anything without earning a fortune. Brickies thought they should be paid like Naomi Campbell and would not get out of bed for less than €1,000 and a breakfast roll. So, the cost of buying land and building on it was no longer a massively cheaper option. Since the recession hit, that relationship has changed back and the cost of building has fallen substantially.

The two most popular ways of approaching a self-build are to use a building contractor, or to employ a project manager. Neither of these is an easy option. When you employ a building contractor, the big worry is that they can hold you to ransom or go bust, leaving you in a difficult situation. You can get a building guarantee which will protect you against structural defects, but it will not be a guarantee that the house is going to be well built. The worst-built property I own has a guarantee.

Basically, building carries as many cons as pros. If you have no experience in the area, if you don't do it correctly, it could be more costly than buying a property. I have built twice and both times, when I looked at all of the costs, I ended up project-managing myself because everyone wants to make a fortune out of you. Each time I finished, I said I would never do it again.

The first time I built I was the project manager and assumed full control of everything. Getting quotes, employing tradespeople, solving problems, buying the raw materials, quantity control, liaising with everyone . . . You can have twenty or thirty people on the site some days, all on top of each other and all telling you why it has to be done their way. It's like the *Krypton Factor* times 1,000. I had never run a site and had not really been on one before, apart from the time I robbed timber and six-inch nails for the cart I was building. I'd done plenty of work on old houses with my dad, so I'm pretty handy if I need to be, but talk about having no experience! I remember ringing my brother-in-law a few days in with a question.

'Here, Paul, what is an ope? I haven't got a clue what it is and I'm being asked about them here.'

Cue about a minute of laughter. 'It's short for opening,' he said.

'Oh, okay.'

It was one of the most difficult projects I have ever undertaken and I would not really recommend it to anyone unless they have contacts in the area. I, fortunately, had my brother-in-law who had built before, and I had access to all of his contacts. I would not fancy going through the Yellow Pages to find people. It could end up costing you more than buying. The second time I built, I employed a project manager to run the site for me. This worked out really well, but success depends entirely on the quality of the manager. They can milk you as well as anyone. Project-managing a building site is a very difficult, time-consuming and skilled job and you need to be excellent at time management. And you can't be a walkover either, because you are definitely going to end up firing at least one person. Being in charge of quality control means that you will be telling people that their work is not good enough plenty of times. If you're a walkover, you will just be handed crap work.

The biggest mistake I ever made when building was agreeing to pay some advisors on a percentage of the build cost as opposed to a flat fee. Never do this. When your advisers are on a percentage of the build cost they may have no interest in reducing costs. They may just see euro signs every time you mention something. Regardless of what they or their professional body tells you is the right amount to pay, ignore them. As far as I can see, these professional bodies are there to help their members make as much money as possible out of the customer. The suggested charges that are given by the professional bodies are used as a bargaining tool. It's always, 'Well, my professional association tells me to charge 11 per cent, so I'll do 9 per cent,' but those rates are always infinitely higher than you can negotiate. And that goes for non-building negotiations, too. Never accept 'I'll do you a good deal.' They never do you a good deal. It's always going to be way higher than if you simply agree a flat price at the start. When you agree a price, everyone knows where they are from the outset, it keeps everyone honest, and when everyone knows what they are going to make out of a project they adjust their work accordingly.

If you're going to do a self-build, be prepared for a tough year, and it may take that long. I worked on my first site from 7 a.m. till 3 p.m. every day, and all day Saturday and Sunday, then worked evenings in the office. This was a bit extreme, but money was tight and I saved everywhere I could, including labouring costs. But I was young and had a shoestring budget, and I still managed to end up with a very high build standard, which I wouldn't have got close to with a contractor. It did, however, nearly kill me.

Your architect won't have the time to oversee day-to-day building and, anyway, it's not his job. Remember, too, that it doesn't matter how experienced the people on site are, you will have to do huge amounts of research. And if you want anything outside the norm, you're the one who's going to have to figure out how to do it. Ten years ago, when I was building, I wanted underfloor heating, curved counter tops, curved walls, a stainless steel staircase, and so on. Sometimes, when you tell them what you want, you would swear you'd asked them to build the Acropolis. But all things considered and as difficult as it is, when it's done right, it can save you hundreds of thousands of euros in building costs. It can allow you to build to a much higher spec than with a contractor. But it's not for the faint-hearted.

Solicitors and Builders

When picking your solicitor, make sure you go to someone who's competitively priced, and make sure, too, that they read the title, which is the legal basis for the ownership of the property. For the past few years, a good number of solicitors were just banging out low-cost conveyancing without fully checking the title for flaws. If there are flaws in the title, you can run into a whole heap of problems when trying to sell. If the buyer's solicitor uncovers a problem, the deal may fall through or you may have to accept a lower sale price. So it's best to get a solicitor recommended to you. If you're stuck, email me and I'll give you someone. And you shouldn't be paying more than €2,500. You need to negotiate as much with the professional classes as with anyone else or you will be cleaned out.

Be careful of apartment blocks built between 2003 and 2008. More than one insurer has just stopped insuring blocks built between these years because a lot of them are beset by problems because of a really poor build quality. Just because a place has Homebond doesn't mean it's well built. I found that out the hard way. An apartment I bought in 2007 was built by, how will I put this? It was built by someone you would not wish to buy anything from. Because it's so poorly built, there are all kinds of problems. My nine-year-old niece could have done a better job. And because of the type of person the builder is (an ignoramus), he fell out with every single tradesperson on the site, so no one will come back and fix anything. They just refuse to have anything to do with him.

Be really careful if you buy off plans. A lot of the measurements are pre-slabbing, so measure it out and make sure it's the same square footage as the plans say it is. If you are buying a parking space, view it first. The same rogue builder sold me a car-parking space that a car can't actually fit in. Check the measurements of everything, because there's very little comeback afterwards. That same builder, by the way, has a project in south county Dublin right now, so approach all new developments with caution.

Find out what kind of person the builder is, especially if you're looking at an estate or apartment complex, because you may have to deal with them for years if they are on the management committee. And, finally, good luck.

11

I Want to Buy Another House

Firstly, and within reason, I think this is a great idea, but it's not for everyone. Owning a rental property can and most probably will wreck your head. If, however, you are looking to boost your pension in twenty to twenty-five years' time with the equivalent of another salary, then it's a great idea and worth the extra work. Most other investments are designed not only to make you money, but also to generate income for the seller. From insurance companies to stockbrokers, the charges on your money are how they get paid. Once you pass any investment to a third party, you have to pay for the privilege. The only way to make proper money is by doing it yourself. And, although it is not popular right now to say it, once you buy right, I still think property is the best investment over a long period of time. It's also the investment your average person can understand best. It gives a monthly return which pays back the mortgage until you own it outright, it's not complicated, it's tangible and, hopefully, its value appreciates as well.

Investment Options

Investment option A: €65,000 is placed on deposit at a rate of 3 per cent (net of tax). Three per cent, it should be said, is a great rate which is available at the moment, but will not be there too long, so I would not expect a return this high over twenty-five years.

Investment option B: €65,000 in a higher-risk fund and giving a net return of 6 per cent after tax. Which is also a high return to expect.

Investment option C: €65,000 used as a deposit to purchase a standard three-bed property.

Purchase price	€260,000
Mortgage amount	€208,000
Monthly mortgage repayment	€1,246 (@ 5.25%)
Mortgage term	25 years
Current monthly rent	€1,200 approx

Total costs:	
Deposit	€52,000
Legal fees	€3,000
Stamp duty	€2,600
Decoration budget	€5,000
Ancillaries	€2,000
Total:	€64,600 (or more)

Expected returns in twenty-five years:

Investment option A: €136,095.50 after tax (money
on deposit @ 3%)

Investment option B: €278,971.43 after tax (fund
with a 6% net return)

Investment option C: Property value €426,557 (assuming 2% price increase per annum)

Or property value €260,000 (if
house prices stay static)

Mortgage amount Nil

Monthly income €1,886.69 (assuming 2% annual increase
in rent per annum)

Or monthly income €1,100–€1,200 (assuming no increases
in rental values)

Even if the value of the property and the rental income
stay static, the fact that you own the property at the end of
the mortgage term gives it the potential to far outweigh any
of the other investments. As far as I'm concerned, if you
pay your mortgage on capital and interest, if you purchase
a decent asset, the best, most secure long-term investment
is property, by a long shot. But, remember, it is work! You
need to let it, you will have vacant periods and will need to
decorate it at least every few years, and you'll have to take
calls, usually at inconvenient times, because something has
broken. But more of that later.

On the downside, the tax you pay for owning an investment property has gone up, and is likely to go up further.
Not only do you have the Non Principal Private Residence

(NPPR) tax of €200 a year and the Private Residential Tenancies Board (PRTB) fee, they've also decreased the amount of relief you can claim for the interest you pay on your mortgage. Up until recently, all of the interest was allowed as a deduction. Now it's only 75 per cent. I wouldn't be surprised if they reduce that amount further, and they will probably bring in another property tax soon also.

You will have to pay tax on the rent you receive, so make sure you keep track of everything you do to the property, because there are a wide range of costs that are tax deductible.

Hassle for Mr John

When I was growing up, in the days before mobile phones, my dad had a few rental properties and the only contact number for tenants was our home number. This meant that if Dad was out, answering the phone was a complete lottery. If it was for you, great. If it was a girl for you, better still, but most likely it was a tenant from a property to say there was some urgent problem like a broken washing machine that needed to be resolved immediately, and no amount of explaining that you were fifteen years of age, six miles away and knew nothing about plumbing could get them off the phone.

For a while, in the eighties, Dad rented to a load of Indian doctors. They always asked for Mr John. If you answered the phone and you got, 'Hello, is that Mr John?' it was a twenty-minute chat about plumbing. This led to us avoiding the phone like the plague if Mum and Dad were out. There could be five kids sitting on the couch watching *The A-Team* while the phone was ringing out beside us.

'I'm not getting it.'

'I got the last one.'

'It's your man looking for Mr John again.'

This did lead to a great game of 'deflecting' with my siblings. If I answered the phone and got caught with a property maintenance call, I'd try and pass it on.

'Hello?'

'Hi, can I speak to Mr John? I'm from building 20 in Rathmines.'

'Yes, certainly, can you hold there for a second? BARRY! THERE'S A GIRL ON THE PHONE FOR YOU!'

My younger brother would come running, wondering who it could be. He'd pick up the phone and hear: 'Hello, Mr John.'

He never thought it was that funny. And to be fair he was upstairs studying to be a doctor while I was outside smoking. Other times, if another brother or my sister had been out and the phone had rung out a load of times, when the absent sibling returned, you'd say, 'You just missed a call. He/she said his/her name was (add appropriate name). He/she said he/she would ring back.'

Then the phone rings and it's answered immediately by someone brimming with teenage anticipation.

'Hello?'

'Hello, Mr John?'

Bull's-eye!

Anyway, my point is that there is work in taking this route. That's the difference between putting money on deposit or investing it in a fund. There is potential for greater returns from property, but it takes work and management and it can be hassle.

You need to find the property, negotiate on the purchase, decorate it, rent it, deal with the upkeep, tenants, vacant periods, interest rate rises and annual tax liabilities. Whereas, when you invest €50,000 in a fund or put it on deposit in the bank, you won't get phone calls from the bank manager on a Saturday night to say a light bulb needs changing or there is a leak in the en suite.

You can limit your exposure to all of this by giving your property management to an estate agent or property management company. For me, it's worth the 10 to 15 per cent they charge to have someone else deal with everything and leave me free to concentrate on my other businesses, but that commission does eat into your income.

Boosting Your Rental Income

There are several things you can do to boost the income from your first investment property. You could, for example, rent out the rooms individually. If you have a three-bed house in a strong market, there is every chance you can increase the rental income by 10 to 20 per cent by doing this. Another good one is to collect the rent every week instead of every month. There are only twelve months in the year, but there are thirteen four-weekly periods, so a weekly collect means you get an extra month. This was something I did for a short while when I was starting out because every penny was needed. As you get older and there is a bit of distance between you and the break-even point, it becomes too much hassle.

You can seriously improve the cash flow if you find a three-bed house with three decent-sized downstairs rooms: a sitting room, a living room and a kitchen area. If the kitchen and living room are big enough, you can convert the other downstairs room into a bedroom and increase the revenue from the house by a substantial amount. If it looks like a duck and quacks like a duck, it's a duck. If the downstairs room has a bed and a wardrobe in it, it's a bedroom.

This is only a runner in a larger house. Those built more recently are terribly small. And increasing the number of bedrooms can reduce the rent you can get for the other rooms because there is less living room. Tenants will weigh everything up.

As with everything else, once you have done something once, the next time will be so much easier. It's the same with buying and decorating property. Renovating a rental property is an entirely different thing to renovating a house you're going to live in, and is worthy of its own book, let alone a chapter.

Once you have found reliable people to use, you can get decoration down to a tee. I have decorated an entire house via a meeting at the back of a van that took about four minutes.

'Yes, those tiles fine, with that carpet, yes, that paint, those wooden floors, those curtains . . . when can you have it finished by?'

Interior designers can both cost you or save you a fortune. A good interior designer is worth their weight in gold, and will even project-manage for you. Apart from the curtains and blinds! Do them yourself! You can save a fortune by buying off-the-shelf curtains and blinds.

One of the mistakes first-time investors make is to confuse decorating the property for rental with decorating it for themselves. They put in everything they would want if they were moving in. You can spend a fortune decorating the property to a high level when, in reality, it makes no difference at all to the rent you'll get from it. That doesn't mean you can't add your own touches to a place. Make sure it looks warm and cosy, with nice colours and all of the basics.

When you're furnishing, there are loads of great value deals out there. Check out the free trade section of *www. dublinwaste.ie*. It's a great place for picking up free stuff. Basically, this site is for people who have furniture and other items that they no longer want and are prepared to give away instead of paying to dump. Having said all that, you need to make sure you don't just put any old crap into the house, as the quality of tenant and the amount of rent you get are directly in proportion to how nice the house looks.

Finance

Securing finance for this type of purchase is a lot more difficult than it used to be. Here's the best way to go about it. When it's only an idea or an intention, you need to start saving. Find out the monthly repayment on the sum you want to borrow and start saving as close to that amount as possible. Don't put €200 here and €200 there and €200 into stock options. Don't confuse the underwriter. You have to make it easy for them to say yes and sign off on it. If your application is complicated, they will say no. Set up a standing order for your savings into another account and do not touch the cash when it gets there. Leave it to build up.

Look for a property to move into as opposed to one to rent out. The banks have separate rules for lending to buy a home and lending to buy an investment property. They will lend you more – up to 90 per cent, generally – and at much better rates, so it will cost you a lot less. If you are buying the same property with the intention of renting it out, you will have more difficulty getting the finance, as they will only lend you a much lower percentage – typically only 75 to 80 per cent, AND they will charge you a much higher rate if you can even get the finance. So, buying your second (or third) property to move into as opposed to a property to rent out is a no-brainer from an affordability point of view. The big variable is whether you are prepared to move house to get the finance.

If you decide to do this again a year or two after, and your plan is to keep going and build up a portfolio, the system is almost the same as when you were buying your first house in Chapter Ten. Make sure that you can show you are able to save at least the amount of the new mortgage repayment. Keep all your payments up to date. Don't overdraw on your bank account if at all possible. Keep your bank accounts and paperwork simple. And, hopefully, in a couple of years' time, the banks will be a little more open to lending on investment properties again.

Choosing the Property

Choosing an investment property is not the same as choosing your own home. If it's a pure rental property, the first consideration is the price and getting a mortgage payment as close to the rental income as possible. The second is public transport. If you are renting the rooms out individually, there is a high likelihood of dependence on public transport. The other consideration is proximity to major employment.

No mention of property could be complete without mentioning these three things: location, location, location! Location will determine how well a property holds its value or appreciates in years to come. The reality is that the better the location, the more expensive the property. As much as I would advise buying the worst house on the best street, rather than the best house on a worse street, you need to do the maths on the more expensive locations, as a lot of the time the mortgage repayment and the rental income may not be as close as in a less expensive area.

It's not always the case, and in a strong market you will make way more from the better location. But with more exclusive properties, the vacant periods can be longer. And the higher mortgage can burn cash way more quickly when unlet.

So, with your first investment property, the key issues are the rental income in the area, public transport and employment. After that, aspect and light, heating, energy rating, build quality, garden and neighbours. I've lived in a property with a poor aspect and you really miss the light. It can feel like winter most of the time. It can be a beautiful day outside and you may not even notice until someone rings and mentions it.

Buying Abroad

I've always been very nervous about buying abroad, although I have done it. It was my third time to the area, I could see the development and the rising economy, and at the time I felt it was early enough in the boom to be worth a punt. What I did, though, was buy on the best street in the place with the best view, where there was high demand and high rental income. My feeling was that there is always demand for the best address even in bad times.

If you are buying abroad, you need to do way more research than if you are buying here. For some reason, people seem to do less. For example, what is the average salary in the country you are looking to buy in? I have heard of people buying in Bulgaria for really high prices, when the average wage was around €300 a month. So who is going to rent your €60,000 apartment for €300 a month? No one local, that's for sure. And even if they do rent it, what are you going to do when they miss a rent payment? And that's in Europe, never mind Mr Wong in your two-bed apartment in Shanghai. No, thanks. It's a bit further than Lucan to go looking for your rent. The thing is to look everywhere, not just in the development or the tourist areas. Otherwise, who will buy your property if you want to sell?

Beware of anyone selling huge gains in value. When people try and rip you off, it's often by appealing to vanity or greed. Beware bus trips to locations. Check the map and go there yourself. You may well be driven all over the place, so you don't see the rough neighbourhoods. You can end up in high-pressure sales environments. These are the hardest sellers around. Never decide on the spot, never succumb to pressure sales. There is no such thing as a free lunch, and anyone paying for your flight is looking for the sale. Make sure you know exactly what you are doing and, once you feel pressure, get out of there and give yourself time to think about it. Spend time in the location, talk to everyone, compare prices with other areas, especially property prices in areas inhabited by locals. Research, research, research.

One of the major issues with buying foreign property is the actual rental income versus the rental income you were sold, particularly on short-term lets. If you do your research and find out that the rental income on the sales literature is inflated even slightly, you can assume everything else is. The property company may tell you that the property is unlet for half the year, while they are pocketing the rent, and you have no way of knowing if it's true or not. I heard of one chap who was told his property was unlet most of the year. He took a trip over to find a blackjack table and card tables in his apartment. There is simply no way to prove the agent is not just pocketing the rental income, especially on short-term rentals.

I realize buying a house in the sun is a dream for many people, but it's such an easy one to get wrong. There are so many countries that I'd be afraid to buy in. In some, there have been instances of illegal building that are now coming back to haunt the purchasers, rather than the developers. I've heard of properties being knocked down, taking people's life savings with them. So, once you've done all of your research, get good legal advice and spend a lot of time there to make sure you know exactly what you're getting into.

Negative Equity

If you have bought a rental property over the past five or six years, you are no doubt in negative equity right now, and may have seen a substantial drop in rental income as well. Every situation is different, so it is impossible to give clear-cut advice on what do to. The haves and the have-nots in this situation are those with tracker rates and those without. Having a tracker rate is so valuable. Being without one means you are without any protection from the bank.

The best way to give advice is through this example, variations of which I've been hearing about all year.

A close friend rang me to ask what she should do about a rental property she bought during the boom. The bank had just written to her to say that if she wanted to keep her tracker rate, she needed to go off interest only and onto capital and interest. The property had dropped in value substantially and the rental income was also down 25 to 30 per cent. So the mortgage was now more than the rent.

Between that, vacant periods between tenants and the usual property maintenance problems, she wanted to know if there was any way of getting rid of it. My advice to her was quite simple. This may be a pain now, but in twenty years' time if you keep paying back the mortgage (interest and capital), you will own the property and the rental income will be a decent bonus to your pension that will pay for your holidays and give you a better quality of life. The unfortunate thing is that because of the drop in rental income, the investment needs some subsidy. But it's not a huge amount. In the long term, I would expect the rental income to increase. I would expect subsidizing the investment property to be a short-term thing only. And, in fact, in the past few months the rental market has started to come back. Rents are going up a little, plus it's taking less time to rent places.

Because of all they read about negative equity, people assume they will never be able to borrow again. But selling the property to get rid of the problem doesn't make sense. Why is it a good idea to sell a property if it goes down in value, but a bad idea to sell it if it goes up in value? Surely it should be the other way around?

If you can't afford to subsidize the tracker, you may have to give it up. If you're paying interest only and can't afford to go capital and interest, the bank may force you onto a higher rate. Remember, if you don't agree with anything your bank dictates, you can complain to the financial ombudsman. His findings are binding and there is no penalty if he does not find for you. One of my customers was told repeatedly by a bank that she was not entitled to her tracker any more, despite the fact that she complained in writing to the bank. She wanted to give up, but I convinced her to go to the ombudsman, and the bank changed its mind in seven days. The difference was €240,000 in interest over the term of the loan. Because there's so much money at stake, they'll say no until you force them into a corner.

If you don't have a tracker rate, you're probably on an expensive variable rate now. My own attitude to all of my own assets is to keep them at all costs. If, however, the rent is less than the mortgage and you can't afford to subsidize, that's a different situation altogether. The most important asset to protect is the family home, along with all the things you need to survive, so you need to write to the bank and tell them about the rental income you're getting, then try to come to some kind of resolution.

12

I Need to Find Low-Risk, High-Yield Investments

If you can find low-risk, high-yield investment opportunities, please let me know. Unfortunately, risk and yield go hand in hand; low risk with low yield and high risk with high yield. It's quite possible to lose all or part of your cash with high-potential-return investments. And these days, even investments that I might have considered zero risk a few years ago, I would classify as low risk now. I can't even say state-guaranteed savings and bank deposits are completely without risk. The most secure place for money has always been American government bonds but, as I write this, they have just lost their AAA rating. There is an argument that money in a bank is maybe less secure than a precious metal like gold or silver. But then again, these particular products have seen huge jumps in value and there is no guarantee that they will stay at these levels. By the time this book comes out, they may even have tanked.

Anyway, one thing I don't want to do is give investment advice, not least because, if you had invested in exactly the opposite way to me since 2007, you would have made a fortune. If you want to understand investment in all its intricate detail, you need to study someone like Warren Buffett, who's had forty or fifty years of getting it right. So, the purpose of this chapter is not to impart investment advice, but to explain how it works. Even if I did want to give tips, they could be shockingly out of date by the time this hits the shelves. So, I will explain the different types of investments that are out there, along with the buzz words, so you'll know what they are, how they work and the risks involved.

As much as I'm going to stay away from investment advice, you know when you really think one area is going to go ballistic and it is on the tip of your tongue, and it's hard to shut up? If you put a gun to my head and told me to pick an investment for a big punt I would have to go with silver. But that investment is not for the faint of heart either. If you look at silver over the years, it goes up and down like a bouncing ball. Last year, it was as low as $12 or $13. As I wrote this, it was $34, but by the time the material was edited it was $42, and a few months later it was back at $29, so going down that road and investing in individual instruments requires constant monitoring. As Warren Buffett said, when he was asked how he got so rich, 'By selling my stocks too early.' Knowing when to get out is as important as knowing when to buy.

Dear Prudence

You need to show prudence when you invest. If you're thinking about getting into higher-risk investments, do your homework, because it can very easily end spectacularly badly. I'm always looking for higher-than-average returns, both within the areas I know about like property and business, and outside those areas in things like unit funds. I invested in some very high-risk products in 2007 that got wiped out. They were down 60 per cent or more. But although high risk, many of these have now recovered. Some of these investments were 'ultra-high risk'. The flip side of these products is that if you get them right, you can make a fortune. Had I gone into them in 2005 or 2008 they would have earned a huge return, assuming I got out in time.

The secret to successful investing is diversity. Spread your investment over a wide range of well-picked instruments, whether you do this yourself or get an adviser or fund manager to do it for you. When I've lost money on investments, it's because I did not do this. By spreading your investment over many areas, you reduce the chances of losing it all or a good part of it. Never have all your eggs in one basket.

I am not the man to advise on how to find good-value stocks to invest in. That's a whole other book with a different author, but there are low-cost ways of investing in stocks and shares (from €5,000 or so upwards), where you decide on the level of risk and a fund manager makes all of the investment decisions. There are a variety of different products to facilitate this, including managed funds, unit-linked funds and tracker bonds, and they are available from life insurance companies, banks and stockbrokers.

Risk

Before you even look at any of these, the first thing to do is to look at yourself and your attitude to risk. Are you interested in low risk only? Or would you consider putting part of your money into medium- or higher-risk investments for potentially higher returns? I mentioned one of the medium-to-high-risk investments to a friend last year. I suggested putting part of her money into a fund because stock markets were making a strong recovery and there was potential for substantial gains.

She asked one question: 'Is there any chance I can lose any of my money?'

'Yes, there is,' I told her, 'it could go down in value.'

'Then I don't like it.'

Fair enough. Discussion over. If you really don't want to take any sort of a chance that the value of your investment may drop, then this type of thing is not for you. The downside of low risk is that the returns are generally poor.

Inflation

In real terms, you can lose money if inflation is higher than the rate you're earning. If it is, your money is effectively going down in value. This can be a bit confusing, so I'll explain it like this. Suppose your monthly grocery bill comes to €100. But next year, prices go up and it costs you

€105. That's inflation at 5 per cent. Now, if your savings on deposit are earning 1 per cent, the next year your €100 with interest is €101. But in year two, your basket of groceries costs €105. So your buying power has fallen by €4. That's inflation eating away at your savings.

Stocks and Shares

It's probably best to start off with the high-risk stuff. If you don't know exactly what you're doing with stocks and shares, your stockbroker is not your friend. You can use a stockbroker's resources to help you, but *you* need to be the decision-maker. If you're doing your own homework and telling the stockbroker what to do and where to invest, he can work for you. If you are not in that category, then stay away, unless you're looking at one of the stockbroker's funds.

A stockbroker, like any other business, has commission targets to meet each and every month, regardless of what the market is doing. For the most part, he doesn't care about you. If you lose money, he won't be thinking about you at the end of the month. He has to justify his salary and, to do that, he has to earn commission. A friend of mine left a stockbroker's during the financial crisis because he had to meet the same commission target at a time when the only sensible advice was to hold tight and do nothing. Stockbrokers earn commission when they buy the stock and, if it goes pear-shaped, they earn commission by selling the same stock. Don't get me wrong, they have their place, and I have used them regularly in the past. The thing is, you need to be using them, not the other way around.

Buying individual stocks is ultra-high risk, regardless of how blue chip the company is. If you get it right, it's brilliant. But if you put your money into individual stocks, you have all of your eggs in one basket. Think of how we viewed Irish banks. We all, me included, thought they were safe as houses. How many people have lost their life savings in bank shares? So many retired people, too. You should never be in a position where you can lose your life savings because a bad chief executive takes control.

But, as risky as an individual stock is, it's nowhere near as risky as borrowing to buy stocks. This is what a CFD does.

Contracts For Difference (CFDs)

Most people hadn't heard of these until Sean Quinn lost everything using them. And this shows just how dangerous they are. One of the country's most successful businessmen got handed his own head on a plate by using CFDs. Effectively, they're like buying shares using a mortgage. But it's a mortgage with a difference. If the value of the shares goes up, everyone is happy. But if they go down, you get a margin call. This is a call to say that because the value of your investment has fallen, you need to increase the money the broker holds as security, or else they'll sell the stock. I remember these calls well from 2007 and 2008. They are not nice calls to get . . .

The benefit of CFDs is that you can buy way more stock than you actually have money for. With €10,000 you can buy, say, €50,000 worth of stock. If the stock goes up 5 per cent, you've made €2,500 – that's a 25 per cent return on your €10,000 investment. The downside is that if the stock plummets, your money is gone. So, if you don't know what you're doing, it's a ticket to the poorhouse.

Spread Betting

Spread betting is full-on gambling. You don't actually own the stock; it's a bet on where the stock will go. The main benefit is that the bet is tax free, plus you can bet on a wide range of stocks and commodities. Spread betting has more in common with futures and options and is even more risky than CFDs. Seasoned pros only, here.

Managed Funds and Unit Trusts

A managed or unit-linked fund is, for my money, the best and lowest-cost way of buying a spread of stocks, shares, commodities or property. You invest in a fund along with thousands of other people. A fund manager then takes the money and, depending on the mandate of that particular fund, invests in a large basket of stocks, shares, cash, government bonds and anything else. They get their slice, too. As with everything in life, the commission they charge is up for negotiation.

Management charges can be anywhere from 0.75 per cent to 2 per cent, so if you can get a 1 per cent rather than a 2 per cent management charge, your investment will make 1 per cent more each year, purely because you negotiated well. Because you can spread your investment over a wide range of investment types, from stocks to property, managed funds have the obvious advantage of spreading the risk.

The best way I can describe a fund as opposed to buying individual stocks is like this: suppose you're at the races and you have €1,000 to gamble. With you are two friends, who are both connected in the racing world and really know their stuff. One of your friends tells you he has a sure thing in the next race and the odds are five to one. He tells you to put all of your money on a win. It's a big gamble but, if it pays off, you walk away with €5,000 profit. Your other friend, an altogether more conservative chap, thinks it's far too risky to put all of your money on one horse. What if it falls at the first hurdle? As good as the horse is, falling at the first is a possibility.

He tells you about his system. He also has €1,000, but he has picked ten horses over the next ten races that he also thinks are sure things. He is putting €50 each way on each horse, so if they come in first, second or third, he wins. With his system, he vastly reduces the chances of losing it all, but he doesn't have the potential upside the first guy has. In return for his spread-the-risk system, he gets 2 per cent of the money you give him to invest.

Spreading the risk is the major benefit of a managed fund. There are many different types out there, from ultra-high to low risk. I personally prefer the signature funds that insurance companies manage, the ones that have been there for years. It's easy to boast about a minor fund when it does well, but it will only have a fraction of the insurance company's money. What about the funds with nearly everyone's money? I don't like giving any company free advertising, but Eagle Star had three main funds when I started in this business twenty years ago: the balanced fund, the performance fund and the dynamic fund. They are still their main funds today, and I expect they will be their main funds in ten years' time. These are the funds I prefer, as opposed to the ones with strange names that you pick out of a thousand.

One fund I keep my eye on is Warren Buffett's Berkshire Hathaway. Why invest myself in areas I'm not strong in when I can get my mate Warren to invest my money in the same way he does?

Commodities

A commodity is a product or a raw material that you can buy in much the same way as you buy a share, and the value of that commodity goes up or down depending on the demand for it. I'm talking about anything from steel and copper to coffee and pork bellies (remember the film *Trading Places*?). They are traded similarly to shares. Knowing how to invest in this area is a full-time job.

Precious Metals

Gold and silver are increasingly being seen as currency again. Up until a few years ago, they actually were currency. Think of the meaning of 'Pound Sterling'. The Gaelic for money is *airgead*. *Airgead* comes from the Latin word for silver – *argentum*. So, in the old days, and not that long ago, paper money represented an amount of precious metal. Up until the 1930s in America, you could walk into any bank, hand in a $20 bill and leave with an ounce of gold. So your paper money represented a precious metal.

It's not so long ago, either, since coins were silver, so people were purchasing items with a precious metal. So, since the world/money/credit crisis, the value of the likes of gold and silver has been rising steadily, because gold, especially, is considered a safe haven in times of turmoil. An ounce of gold is trading at about €1,100 as I write, enough to buy you a nice, tailor-made suit. It's interesting to note that in Roman times an ounce of gold would also buy you a nice tailor-made suit . . .

Gold and silver have been on a big run. They are both worth way more than they were a year or two ago. Have they finished their run? Have they a long way to go, or will they drop? They do trade very turbulently, but there are compelling arguments in favour of holding some precious metals, because of their finite supply. Silver, in particular, has an end-use in technology, as opposed to gold, which is reused and reused. You can also buy gold easily enough in coins or bars, in insurance company funds or Exchange Traded Funds (ETFs).

But the same diversification principle applies. Even the people who sell the stuff will tell you never to have any more than 10 per cent of your money in gold or precious metals.

Exchange Traded Fund (ETF)

Have you ever heard about the monkey and the fund manager? It does the rounds every so often: a fund manager is pitted against a monkey, who randomly picks stocks by throwing darts at a board. Surprisingly enough, the monkey wins a lot. Why, then, are we paying fund managers to actively pick stocks for us?

While a fund manager actively trades stocks, an ETF can be used to track an index like the Dow Jones. So, if you were to buy into an ETF, you would be buying into the whole index rather than an individual stock or share. Suppose you invest €10,000 into the Dow Jones when it's at 10,000. When they tell you on the news that the Dow is up 300 points to 10,300, your €10,000 is now worth €10,300. ETFs can also allow you to trade other commodities, sectors and precious metals and are available from stockbrokers.

Currency

This is one of those areas I wish I'd studied a bit more this year. Two things I want to get into as soon as I have some time off are Texas Hold'Em and currencies. We've all been listening to the news for years and heard about the yen and the euro and Sterling, and so on. So, the year before last, a euro was worth 97 pence. If you had transferred €1,000 to Sterling and then back again when the value of the euro dropped to 84 pence, you would have made about 15 per cent. Not bad. But you would need to use a broker for this because bank charges would negate the gains.

Hedge Funds

Hedge funds are privately managed funds, which are usually aimed at high-net-worth individuals. They invest in a wide array of areas from currency to stocks, and can be either long or short on whatever they invest in. The term 'long' means that it is bought in the hope it goes up in value. Effectively, 'long' is a buzz word for just owning a share or other investment. You're probably familiar with the term 'short selling', since the practice of short selling bank shares was stopped a couple of years ago.

Short selling happens when you sell a stock that you don't own, and if it goes down, you can then buy it back at the lower price, making a profit. You may be asking how you can sell a share you don't own and the answer is, you borrow it. As with nearly everything you borrow, once you borrow it you owe it back. So if, when you have to return the stock, you can buy it back for lower than you sold it, there is your profit. It's exactly the opposite of buying a share in the expectation it will go up. The downside of short selling is that if the stock goes up, you could face a pretty big loss and, unless you sell, this can turn into an unlimited loss. If you're looking at a hedge fund, make sure it's regulated, check out what areas they invest in, and have a good read of their prospectus to make sure you're happy with their products. They implement various strategies, and their intention is to return higher-than-average performance and have, as the name suggests, a hedge against a downturn in the market.

Money on Deposit

This has traditionally been the safe-as-houses model, but that has all been turned on its head in the past few years by a reckless few. All money in Irish banks is guaranteed by the state under two different schemes. The rates on offer from banks which are in dire need of deposits can be as high as 3.6 per cent. That's great value. When you consider they are also lending money out on tracker rates at 2 per cent, it doesn't take a mathematical genius to work out there's a problem there.

Bank deposits are what we would call low risk. This is where your money goes if you don't want to risk any of it at all. You need to shop around each year, or even every six months for the best options. Despite the good rates that are out there, many people have money on deposit with the banks at 0.1 per cent which, given inflation of over 2 per cent, means their money is losing value. The other option is the Post Office which, of course, is free from Dirt Tax.

If you want to compare the rate of interest you get from the Post Office with what you get from the bank, just use a calculator to add the interest rate to your savings amount and, in the case of the bank, just knock 27 per cent off the interest bill. Then compare the net amounts. The banks can still beat the Post Office for returns, even after Dirt Tax.

Government Bonds

If you're giving the government money through the Post Office, why not take out a government bond instead, and get ten times the rate? You can buy government bonds through a stockbroker. Although they are guaranteed by the same people, I can't see the government defaulting on Post Office rates. But government bonds? That's a different story. Great returns, but high risk.

Vintage Cars and Fine Art

The only investment I made that went up in value in 2007 was my vintage cars. When everything else was falling down around me, vintage cars were actually doing well. If I had held onto them, they would have been up another 30 per cent or so since then. Once you pick right, vintage cars can be a great investment. When markets get tough, classic cars don't follow the same pattern as stocks, and money can flow into them rather than out of them.

Tracker Bonds

I'm not really sure I like tracker bonds. I've seen many of them give returns way lower than were expected. There are, however, companies with good pedigrees in this area, so if you want to invest in the stock market but don't want to risk your capital, they are an option. Before you get involved, ask to see the performance of all of that company's tracker bonds.

They work like this: a part of your investment is put on deposit with a bank and interest is paid on that deposit. So, if you are investing €10,000, €9,000 goes on deposit. That €9,000 earns €1,000 interest, which gives you €10,000 at the end of the term. That's how your original investment is guaranteed. The other €1,000 then buys options on whatever you're investing in; that's the part that does the work.

There are restrictions, so you should read the small print, or get it read by someone who knows their stuff. I would prefer to divide and manage my money myself; put 80 to 90 per cent on deposit, and 10 or 20 per cent into a higher-risk fund – say, a well-picked managed fund or similar. But that's not to say a tracker bond is not for you if you want a simple investment which gives potential gains from the stock market. As with everything else, speak to as many people as you can, collect your information and make an informed decision. Considering the amount of time and hard work it takes to get your lump sum together, spending a bit of time working out how to make it work for you should be a priority.

Advice

There are great advisers, average advisers and bad advisers, and there are so many different types of investments out there, too, that it is difficult to know who to take advice from. Remember, any adviser can only give advice on the products he is regulated to sell. So, it's really up to you to decide who to take advice from. The best way of doing that is by speaking to plenty of people, until you find someone whose advice you are happy with. Just be sure to spread the risk.

I spoke to someone whose adviser got them to move their pension funds and savings out of stocks and into gold three years ago. That turned out to be as good advice as you can get. One stockbroker told me not to put any money into the market in 2007, and another one seemed to ring me every Friday when he had a target to hit. His only motivation was hitting his targets, not giving good advice. So, when you get someone who you trust, hold onto them.

Savings

There's a good chance you're reading this and going, that's all well and good but I've no money to invest, so it's no use to me! Investment is the best way of making money. To get there, you need money, and to get there, you need a savings plan.

Saving ad-hoc amounts is really not the way forward.

Instead, you need to decide on a set amount that you can't touch that goes out of your account by direct debit each month. There are a number of products you can use to make this happen. A straightforward membership of a credit union or a bank savings account is perfect. Insurance companies also arrange savings plans that are a lot more client-friendly than they used to be. For years, the only real winners out of savings plans were the salesperson and the insurance company, because the charges were so high. There are now low-commission options which allow you to invest in the stock markets via managed funds, much like the Special Savings Incentive Account (SSIA) savings plans, though without the tax break. Make sure you're happy with the charges and commission, and with the level of risk you want to expose yourself to. These products may be the way to go if you're looking for higher returns than on deposit, but if you want very low risk, the credit union or bank savings plan are the best options.

It's really important to get into the discipline of saving. Whenever you get a pay rise, you should put part of it into a savings plan. Otherwise, you'll just adjust your spending to your new salary and won't make any progress. That used to happen to me. I'd think that it was all going to change with a raise, but my spending just adapted to my new budget, so my money went into the black hole that was my current account. You need to have your rainy day money. Thank God for rainy day money. If I hadn't got my rainy day money, I would not have written this, because I would have been bankrupt in 2010. You never know what you might need it for, from college fees to emergencies. Money makes money, but the hard part, as with everything else, is the first few steps.

13

I Need to Protect What I've Got

Why would anyone in their right mind buy life assurance? It costs a decent chunk of money every month, and it's only paid out when you die! Why would you want to pay for something like that? You wouldn't, well, not for yourself, anyway, and that's the point of life cover. You see, life cover is not for the person who's insured, life cover is bought to provide for everyone else in your life. It's there to make sure that there are no mortgages or loans left behind, and to replace your salary or income to allow your family to continue to live comfortably. Life cover is the most unselfish purchase a person can make. For the same price as Sky Sports 1, 2 and 3, and all of the movie channels, you get . . . absolutely nothing . . . for you.

So, if your fella never buys you flowers, but has taken out a decent policy to make sure you will always be secure, give him a bit of leeway, as he's probably spending more each month on life cover than a big bunch of roses costs, but without any of the immediate benefits. If you're single with no dependants, you need very little cover, and if you have some savings, none at all, unless you have a mortgage. But if you have dependants and no life cover, quietly mark your place in this book, close it and firmly hit yourself on the forehead with it. If you have a mortgage, you no doubt have mortgage protection. Mortgage protection is another way of saying life insurance. The only difference is that, instead of the life cover staying at the amount you took out, it reduces each year in line with what you pay back on the mortgage. So you could start with €200,000 worth of cover in year one, then in year two it's down to €196,000, and so on, until you're at nil in the final month.

How Much Cover do You Need?

To work out how much life cover you need, you simply have to take your salary and multiply it by the number of years left until your dependants are no longer dependent. So, for example, suppose you have one child aged three and you earn €45,000 per annum. You need to replace your income until he or she has finished college, say that's in twenty years' time. So the cover you need is €45,000 times twenty, which comes to €900,000, plus insurance to cover all loans. You may also have life insurance cover as part of your company pension plan. If so, simply deduct that level of cover from the €900,000 to give you the ideal amount. Sounds like a lot, doesn't it? And then you need to do the same for your partner.

It may be, however, that this level of cover is unaffordable right now. If that is the case, which is most of the time these days, work out what you need per year until your youngest is not a dependant any more, and deduct the life cover you already have for your mortgages and loans. If that is still unaffordable, then just decide on what you can afford to pay each month and get as much cover as possible with the premium you can afford; maybe price a shorter term. The reality is that this is what happens in nearly every case. Go for as much cover as you can get for the money you have allocated for insurance, then review it in a couple of years when things are a little better. If you can only afford €20 a month, take out a policy for that. Just don't go uncovered. Even €20 can go a long way with life cover.

Your financial situation and your needs and wants are continuously changing. That's why you should look at all of this stuff on a yearly basis.

What to Buy

There are a few different types of life insurance. The main ones are term insurance and what is called 'whole of life'. Term insurance is just like your car insurance, except instead of being for one year, it's for ten or twenty years. The whole of life plan is an open-ended insurance plan. There are variations of this type of plan. However, the most common plan is a unit-linked whole of life plan. How it works is, the money you pay each month goes into an investment fund, and each month the cost of life cover is deducted. The principle is that the growth of your investment goes some way towards covering the cost of your life cover, which gets more expensive as you grow older. The issue with this type of cover is that the insurance company decides what the cost is. The premiums are not guaranteed and can be reviewed and increased at regular intervals. So, my personal preference is term cover. It's cheaper and guaranteed throughout the contract.

I'm not a big fan of whole of life insurance because, a lot of the time, it ends up costing too much. With term insurance, there's no ambiguity. It costs this much for this many years, full stop. You could chat to another adviser who might have a whole different opinion, but I always like to know what everything costs in advance and for what term. That way there are no surprises and everyone knows what they get. If you are taking out term insurance, always build in what is called a 'conversion option'. This means that at the end of the term you can convert it into another policy, without giving any medical evidence. That bit is really important, so don't forget!

Serious Illness Cover

If life cover is for everyone else in your life, serious illness cover is for you. Serious illness cover, or what is now called specified illness cover, is a relatively modern insurance. As a result of advances in medicine, when you have a serious illness, you are very likely to be alive for years and years. Not so long ago these illnesses were more likely to be terminal.

If you are unfortunate enough to suffer a serious illness like one of the cancers covered, you may be out of work for a year or more and, in that time, you'll have the mortgage to pay and all of the normal financial matters to take care of. Specified/serious illness cover pays out a lump sum if you are hit by one of the illnesses covered under your policy. This is insurance for living. How many people do you know who have been hit by cancer or heart attack and are alive many years later? If that were to happen to you, wouldn't it be great to have the mortgage cleared? Or to have a cash lump sum to take the financial pressure off or help with convalescence? The last thing you want is to have financial worries on top of health worries.

The problem with this type of insurance is it's expensive, especially if you're a smoker. I have millions in life cover, but the one I would not let drop is the serious illness cover. Which reminds me, I'm off the smokes more than a year; I must top up my own cover . . .

The cheapest way of getting cover for a decent term is by making your mortgage protection policy include serious illness. As this is decreasing cover, you can get high cover substantially cheaper than level term insurance (where the cover does not go down).

Income and Payment Protection

Here are two types of insurance that people mix up a lot, for obvious reasons. Income protection insures your salary, so if you are unable to work, the insurance company will pay you a monthly salary until your retirement age. A period of between eight weeks and one year must elapse before the insurance company starts paying out. If you already have this kind of cover with your work, you can take out further income protection insurance, to begin once your work cover has ended.

One of the benefits of this type of insurance is that you get tax relief, so you can get up to half of the premiums back in tax breaks. The cost will depend on when you want protection to start. Eight weeks after you've been forced out of work will cost a lot more than a year.

As with all insurance, the more you need, the more expensive it becomes, and if you're in one of those occupations, like drivers, with high instances of claims, you may find it impossible to get.

Payment protection pays you a set amount after four weeks for no more than twelve months. It covers you for both illness and redundancy. The big difference between income protection and payment protection is that the latter is for a year only and it covers redundancy. It's generally sold with your mortgage. If you can't get income protection, payment protection may be an option, but the large number of redundancies recently has forced its cost up, making it a lot less attractive. And beware, some people have taken out payment protection, claimed on it, and discovered something in the small print which revealed that they were never covered at all.

Car Insurance

Out of all of the insurances, the one we hate buying most is car insurance. It's probably ingrained in us because we all got taken to the cleaners when we went to insure our first car.

'Hi, can I get a quote for car insurance, please?'

'Certainly sir, what age are you?'

'Twenty-two.'

'Yes, we would be delighted to do that for you. The price is €4,949.87, and you can pay in instalments over seven months.'

'AGH!'

I sold my Triumph Spitfire to go to the World Cup in 1994. Five months later, I became self-employed. I needed a proper car and bought a Renault Clio. I was twenty-two and the insurance was £2,300. Paying it over was like giving away a kidney, and that price was quite reasonable at the time, compared to some of the other quotes. I'm obviously paying way less now, but the downside is you know you're getting old when your car insurance is cheap!

Although it will always be more expensive for younger drivers, it's not half as bad as it used to be, because now there are specialist insurers who will cover them. So, it's just a case of making sure you talk to a broker who specializes in insuring young drivers.

There is no great secret to car insurance. Because it's a grudge buy, some people would drive across the country to save a fiver. We're all trying to recoup the losses of a five-grand premium twenty years ago. You just need to shop around each year, and if you are considering moving to another insurer, check the policy details, because they are not all the same. Make sure you get bonus protection, if at all affordable. And, like everything else in life, you won't get a discount unless you ask.

Home Insurance

With home insurance, you get what you pay for. The difference between the most expensive and the cheapest can be enormous. Some of the cheaper plans really are stripped-out versions, so you need to check what is covered and compare. Some policies have accidental damage and others don't. In this climate, the extra cover can be a luxury and may be discarded for a cheaper premium, but just be sure you know what you are buying.

Never let your home cover lapse. As every penny is a prisoner right now, people are getting rid of anything non-essential. Home insurance is not a non-essential. Regardless of how tight things are, get minimum cover.

If you are right at the limit of your rebuilding cost, make sure the policy you take out does not have what is called in insurance-speak the 'average clause'. The average clause means, if you are underinsured and you claim, your claim will be reduced by whatever amount you are under-insured by. For example, suppose your house is insured for €100,000 and you have to claim. The assessor says that the rebuilding cost is €120,000. If your policy has an average clause, the insurer can say you are underinsured by 20 per cent, so they can reduce the €100,000 claim by 20 per cent and only pay €80,000.

Never let your home insurance lapse. And if you do have to go for basic cover and end up at the bare minimum of cover, just make sure there is no average clause.

Good Luck

So, anyway, that's it. I'm sitting at the bar in Dax finishing the last chapter and have just ordered a glass of wine. My editor told me a while ago that when I got this over to her, I would have written my first book. Jaysus, I'll leave the writing alone for a while. It took a lot longer than I thought. If you're still reading now, that might mean I've done the job I set out to, which was to try and write a finance book that would not bore you to tears, unless, of course, you started reading this a year ago . . . So thanks for reading, I hope you've learned something from it; more from my mistakes than anything. It's from those that I've learned the most.

Writing a book takes a whole lot longer than you would think! As part of the final edit, months after I wrote the paragraph above, I had to read over the book from start to finish. I'd love to change a few things. Reading your own words about a tough part of your life is cringeworthy at the best of times. More important, time changes your attitude to so much – some of this was written almost a year ago when my confidence was at an all-time low. But a year is a long time and it's amazing how things can change in just twelve months. I wrote those early chapters when all of the feelings were still raw and recent, so I've decided not to alter them. But I am delighted to report that my businesses and companies are going from strength to strength – monthly turnover, gross profit and staff numbers are all now way more than they were at the height of the boom, and more than I could have imagined when I set out to write this book.

So my final message is to keep the faith – sometimes success can just be as simple as hanging in there the longest.

Acknowledgements

There are a few people I want to say thanks to. The first are my girlfriend Karen, my brother Mike and Mr Conor Galvin. Thanks for the help and support when it all turned upside down. And for sticking with me and dragging me out to play when I was a pain in the hole to be around. It made a huge difference to me. Thanks a million to Dad, Mum and my other siblings Barry, Hugh and Caitriona, for their support over the years. You have always been my best salespeople.

Thanks also to Donal and Mark Atkins, Mark O'Byrne and John Hearn for all your help with the book, to my agents Niamh Kirwin and Noel Kelly, and to Patricia Deevy and Michael McLoughlin at Penguin for allowing me extensions on my homework, for asking me to write in the first place and for all their advice (they may have had to coax and push me more than their average author).

Thanks a million to everyone who has worked for me over the past ten years, from Suzanne – my first employee in the mortgage game – to Rob Murphy – my last in the mortgage game – and (nearly) everyone in between. Thanks for your loyalty over the years that allowed the companies to grow so quickly. Thanks also to my fellow owners, directors and managers in Quotedevil.ie, Pembroke Insurance, First Credit Assurance and Dax Café Bar: Graham, Paul, Francis, Olivier, Lesleyanne Saq and all 40ish employees. And, finally, thanks to Mr Martin Codyre, a man who shows determination in the face of adversity and has a truly inspirational attitude.